Economic Actors, Economic Behaviors, and Presidential Leadership

Lexington Studies in Political Communication

Series Editor: Robert E. Denton, Jr.,
Virginia Polytechnic Institute and State University

This series encourages focused work examining the role and function of communication in the realm of politics including campaigns and elections, media, and political institutions.

RECENT TITLES IN THE SERIES:

Almost Madam President: Why Hillary Clinton "Won" in 2008, By Nichola D. Gutgold
Communicator-in-Chief: How Barack Obama Used New Media Technology to Win the White House, Edited by John Allen Hendricks and Robert E. Denton, Jr.
Centrist Rhetoric: The Production of Political Transcendence in the Clinton Presidency, By Antonio de Velasco
Us against Them: The Political Culture of Talk Radio, By Randy Bobbitt
Studies of Identity in the 2008 Presidential Campaign, Edited by Robert E. Denton, Jr.
Internet Policy in China: A Field Study of Internet Cafés, By Helen Sun
Campaign Finance Reform: The Political Shell Game, By Melissa M. Smith, Glenda C. Williams, Larry Powell, and Gary A. Copeland
The Perfect Response: Studies of the Rhetorical Personality, By Gary C. Woodward
A Communication Universe: Manifestations of Meaning, Stagings of Significance, By Igor E. Klyukanov
Presidential Campaign Rhetoric in an Age of Confessional Politics, By Brian T. Kaylor
Manipulating Images: World War II Mobilization of Women through Magazine Advertising, By Tawnya J. Adkins Covert
The Politics of Style and the Style of Politics, Edited by Barry Brummett
Communication Realities in a "Post-Racial" Society: What the U.S. Public Really Thinks about Barack Obama, By Mark P. Orbe
Politics and the Twitter Revolution: How Tweets Influence the Relationship between Political Leaders and the Public, By John H. Parmelee and Shannon L. Bichard
The Rhetoric of Soft Power: Public Diplomacy in Global Contexts, By Craig Hayden
Coming to Terms: The Collected Works of Jane Blankenship, Edited by Janette K. Muir
Reelpolitik Ideologies in American Political Film, By Beverly Merrill Kelley
Media Bias in Presidential Election Coverage 1948–2008: Evaluation via Formal Measurement, By David W. D'Alessio
Gender and the American Presidency: Nine Presidential Women and the Barriers They Faced, By Theodore F. Sheckels, Nichola D. Gutgold, and Diana Bartelli Carlin
The George W. Bush Presidency: A Rhetorical Perspective, Edited by Robert E. Denton, Jr.
New Media, Old Regimes: Case Studies in Comparative Communication Law and Policy, By Lyombe S. Eko
Culture, Social Class, and Race in Public Relations: Perspectives and Applications, Edited by Damion Waymer
Purpose, Practice, and Pedagogy in Rhetorical Criticism, Edited by Jim A. Kuypers
Dark Money, Super PACs, and the 2012 Election, By Melissa M. Smith and Larry Powell
The Rhetoric of Genocide: Death as a Text, By Ben Voth
Studies of Communication in the 2012 Presidential campaign, Edited by Robert E. Denton, Jr.
Economic Actors, Economic Behaviors, and Presidential Leadership: The Constrained Effects of Rhetoric, By C. Damien Arthur

Economic Actors, Economic Behaviors, and Presidential Leadership

The Constrained Effects of Rhetoric

C. Damien Arthur

LEXINGTON BOOKS
Lanham • Boulder • New York • London

Published by Lexington Books
An imprint of The Rowman & Littlefield Publishing Group, Inc.
4501 Forbes Boulevard, Suite 200, Lanham, Maryland 20706
www.rowman.com

16 Carlisle Street, London W1D 3BT, United Kingdom

British Library Cataloguing in Publication Information Available

Library of Congress Cataloging-in-Publication Data Available
ISBN 978-0-7391-8783-8 (cloth : alk. paper)
ISBN 978-0-7391-8784-5 (electronic)

∞™ The paper used in this publication meets the minimum requirements of American National Standard for Information Sciences—Permanence of Paper for Printed Library Materials, ANSI/NISO Z39.48-1992.

Printed in the United States of America

To first-generation, low-income students . . .

Contents

List of Figures

List of Tables

Acknowledgments

Completing an empirical manuscript in political science is no easy task for an individual. It takes a significant amount of work, dedication, and, most importantly, collaboration with others. Therefore, I must recognize the help of many other individuals, whether they provided support that helped my work or encouragement of my commitment to it. Their contributions and support were instrumental in this undertaking and deserve mention. Even though the words pale in comparison, thank you for everything—as insignificant as it sounds.

I must acknowledge Robert E. Denton, PhD, the series editor for Lexington Studies in Political Communication. He was incredibly helpful and supportive during the process. Moreover, I must thank him for having faith and confidence in my work, especially since I am a new scholar and faculty member. For this, I am grateful.

I would like to mention a few specific individuals who made this original research and small contribution to knowledge possible. The foremost has to be Robert DiClerico, PhD, who chaired my dissertation committee. His passion for the presidency, his Socratic-method approach to teaching, and his legendary seminar on the American presidency cultivated my interest in the president and engendered in me the desire to use my dissertation to learn more about this area of research. He is the quintessential professor: rigorous, engaging, and challenging as well as friendly and approachable. I will continuously strive to emulate him as a scholar, professor, and academician. He provided guidance, questions, and comments that enhanced this research and enabled me to think about the presidency as would a serious scholar. Dr. DiClerico's fastidious and meticulous approach to the use of language has, without doubt, made this a better and more readable piece of research.

It is to my wife, Joni R. Magnusson, that I owe the most thanks. She always provided the type of support I needed to keep me sane and focused. She is, without a doubt, the smartest, most beautiful, and most determined individual I have ever met. I have never seen a person work harder than she does. Over the years, this attitude and perspective has motivated me to be the same way. I am forever grateful for her presence in my life. Her ability to help me clarify my scattered ideas and her consistent willingness to be patient with the subject matter, and my feeble attempt at explaining it, are nothing short of saintly.

I would like to thank my daughter Sophia Katherine, an incarnation of pure joy and happiness. Her smile is illuminating and life-changing. While writing, I saw her develop from a newborn to a toddler. I will never forget the many nights she slept on my chest as I wrote. Her mere presence was motivating and inspiring. I am so proud of her. I thought that the day she was born was the most amazing day of my life; every day since then, however, has been more rewarding and fulfilling. Being Sophie's dad is the most humbling, greatest privilege and honor I have ever experienced. I love her so much, and I look forward to the many more years we have ahead of us as a family.

Prolegomenon

> Presidential power is the power to persuade . . .
>
> —Richard Neustadt (1991)

The importance of the economy in American politics cannot be overstated. Except during times of national military conflicts, the public thinks the economy is the most important issue (Wood, 2007). Therefore, presenting an accurate image of the economy to the public is essential for a president (Abramowitz, 2008). If he misconstrues the condition of the economy, it damages his image as an economic leader and the public will often hold him accountable; this is also true for those vying to be president (Hoffman and Howard, 2010; Vavreck, 2009; Wood, 2007). Such a balancing act makes leading the public difficult for presidents, particularly during economic downturns (Cohen and Hamman, 2003; Hoffman and Howard, 2010).

During the 2008 U.S. presidential campaign, the economy became severely unstable in September, particularly with the collapse of Lehman Brothers—which caused a massive ripple effect throughout many of the economy's indicators: unemployment, home values, inflation, stock market, gross domestic product (GDP), and consumer confidence (Abramowitz, 2008; Beck, 2009). The public mood and institutions seemed to be bracing for another Great Depression. Accordingly, as a result of external expectations and a leadership opportunity, the candidates offered their perspective on the economic crisis, namely, how the government should intervene.

In response to the economic situation, the Republican Party's nominee, John McCain said, "The fundamentals of our economy are strong" (Woolley and Peters, 2014—"Barack Obama, 2008") on September 15, the day Lehman Brothers filed for bankruptcy and the Dow Jones dropped nearly five hundred points. Unfortunately, for him, his statement landed outside of the public's expectations for presidential leadership on the economy. In fact, Senator McCain had to later backtrack and offer clarifying remarks about his earlier statement. The Democratic Party's nominee, Barack Obama responded with a specific narrative, wherein he framed Senator McCain as "out of touch" with the mainstream American public and their expectations regarding the president and his responsibility toward the economy (Abramowitz, 2008). Senator Obama claimed that Senator McCain's comment was evidence of his Republican boilerplate economic ideology and policy, which put the American people in this economic situation—he could not be trusted with the responsibility he sought (Abramowitz, 2008).

After both major party candidates were chosen, Senator Obama led the polls most of the time. However, beginning on September 7, 2008, Senator McCain took a one-point lead over Senator Obama in the *Real Clear Politics* poll average. McCain's lead actually continued to grow—at one point his lead was as high as 2.9 points. Within a day of McCain's statement, the two candidates were tied. In the following days, Senator McCain's poll numbers continued to decline. In fact, within a month, he was down by as much as eight points (Abramowitz, 2008).

As we all know how the election turned out, it seems as though the American people agreed with Senator Obama's assessment of McCain's economic leadership potential (Beck, 2009). The economic situation became the focus for the rest of the campaign. By the end of October 2008, the economy was the most important issue on the minds of voters, topping both the War in Iraq and energy—both important in previous polls (Beck, 2009). Moreover, most major polls indicated that the public had a greater confidence in Senator Obama's ability to handle the economy over Senator McCain.

Obviously, there are other issues at stake in a national presidential election (Abramowitz, 2008). Nevertheless, the economy was vastly important to those that voted (Beck, 2009). And, Senator McCain's inability to convince the public that his leadership approach was superior to Senator Obama's facilitated in his defeat for the presidency in 2008 (Beck, 2009). In addition, the "economic leadership" style and image that Senator Obama pursued worked. He was able to paint himself as connected to the people, their needs, and concerns as opposed to a government official bearing partial responsibility for the crisis.

Senator Obama understood the importance the public placed in economic leadership and the perception of the economy that needed to be projected. He pursued this campaign strategy successfully. More importantly, however, is that he did not stop with the strategy at the end of the campaign. As president-elect, he continued to shape his "economic rhetoric" according to public expectations. For instance, President Obama mentioned the "economy" within two minutes of his Inaugural Address—calling it "a concern that rises above all others, and rightly so" (Woolley and Peters, 2014—"Inaugural," 2009). A few sentences later, he offers "hope" rather than a principled declaration of the "fundamentals of our economy." There is no disillusion regarding what he thinks about the state of the economy when he says, "We will rebuild, we will recover, and the United States of America will emerge stronger than before" (Woolley and Peters, 2014—"Inaugural," 2009). In fact, according this research, he does not speak positively about the economy until September 2009, which is nearly a year after taking office—his comments are either negative or neutral. At the time of writing this, President Obama had mentioned the "economy" in 1,913 speeches or documents out of a total of 4,826 opportunities, which is 40 percent of his total presidential rhetoric. It seems as though President Obama always maintains what he thinks is the appropriate balance with 21 percent positive economic statements, 43 percent negative economic statements, and 36 percent neutral economic statements, which matches what Gallup Polls reflect, namely, the public's positive perceptions of the economy fluctuate between 25 percent and 15 percent and while poor perceptions hover around 40 percent (Gallup, 2014).

Presidential Responsibility and the Economy

The evolution of multiple policy institutions and legal mandates that deal with economic issues have altered presidential responsibilities related to the economy (Wood, 2007). The increasing pressures and responsibilities of presidential oversight for the economy have forced the president to devote more time and resources to the economy—more than any other issue besides national security (Edwards and Wayne, 1985; Wood, 2007). Moreover, in response to the external expectations, presidents have increased their promises about what they will accomplish economically. This has compelled presidents to increase their staff and institutional support for economic policymaking, particularly after the Great Depression (Dolan, Frendreis, and Tatalovich, 2008).

The increased expectations for what the president should do with regard to the economy as well as the increased presidential attention to the economy have created more expectations. Namely, considering the responsibility that the president has to the economy and the amount of time and resources he devotes to it, he should be able to influence what happens in the economy. There are substantial scholarly disagreements, however, about the extent to and manner in which the president influences the economy. Mainly, the questions center around whether or not the president's influence is direct, indirect, or nonexistent, and more importantly, how his rhetoric facilitates in meeting the aforementioned expectations—does it function as a powerful mechanism of persuasion and leadership or does it simply placate constituencies?

Some scholars argue that the president's ability to shape the economy should be substantiated by the fact that he is the foremost person with economic information, which makes him the most visible figure present in economic discussions (Eshbaugh-Soha, 2006; Wood, 2007). The fact that the president has the largest staff of economic actors providing him with information and advice makes him appear to be the preeminent economic policymaker. Moreover, the president is the figure the public holds most accountable for the state of the economy (Vavreck, 2009; Wood, 2004). This unparalleled role gives him a profound and direct influence over the economy; those involved in determining the economy's variability, outcomes, and indicators look to the president for information, guidance, and leadership. In short, his policy rhetoric provides the direction and guidance that persuades and influences the behavior and decision-making of the most pertinent economic actors.

For the president to have a direct effect upon economic indicators he needs to garner an acceptable response from each economic actor; to assume that this would happen is suspect. Even if all of the conditions explicated by Neustadt (1991) exist when the president is discussing the economy, the argument that presidential rhetoric influences the economy fails to factor in the possibility that the economic actors are not listening or have agendas of their own that are contrary to the president (Edwards, 2003; Fenno, 1973; Jacobs and Shapiro, 2000; Smith and Deering, 1990).

The argument assumes that economic actors are waiting to hear from the president about what economic decisions they should make. It also assumes that they can be persuaded to change their minds about how they had previously decided to act rather than acknowledging that they rarely if ever listen to and agree with the president (Edwards, 1983; 2003; Krehbiel, 1991; Light, 1999; Lowi, 1985). Moreover, the assertion does not take into consideration that there are externalities affecting presidential agendas, such as resources, political capital, and public approval as well as electoral margin and reputation (Light, 1999). In fact, most of the resources are incredibly scarce; resources are essential to presidential agendas, but yet they begin to decline immediately upon assuming the presidency, leaving the presidents less effective and less influential with regard to the economic actors. The circumstances needed for presidents to shape the economy as a result of rhetoric are not likely to happen; the externalities involved in the political process and the externalities over which the president has little control can become insurmountable.

Therefore, this analysis contributes to the literature by pointing out the limitations of the president's ability to use rhetoric to influence the decisions of economic actors. This objective is accomplished by analyzing the president's public speeches on the economy, how the audiences respond to that rhetoric, assuming they hear/encounter it, and the externalities that must be considered when analyzing the effect of presidential rhetoric on the economy, using different data sets than previously used. There is no definitive argument in the literature explicating the limitations of presidential rhetoric influencing others to take actions on the economy. There is an assumption that what presidents say matters rather than a comprehensive empirical determination of whether such claims can be substantiated. Does the rhetoric engender substantive actions or are presidents' decisions to address the economy so often an institutional necessity? A more comprehensive empirical assessment shows the extent to which presidential rhetoric can predict the behavior of the economic actors; it determines if the rhetoric matters in the way that some of the literature suggests.

According to this research, the presence of presidential rhetoric, aggregated expressions of positivity and negativity, does not, significantly, predict changes in economic actor behaviors. Using presidential statements regarding the economy from Harry S. Truman through Barack Obama (1946–2012), this book analyzed the president's relationships with some of the most salient economic actors (the Federal Reserve [Fed], the public, and Congress), and found that presidents are not successful, overall, at shaping the behaviors of economic actors with their rhetoric. The research suggests that these economic actors have their own goals and perspectives, and, even though presidents have increased their responsibilities toward the economy and maximized their rhetoric regarding the economy significantly, these increases in rhetoric, responsibility, and attention to the economy have not created the desired effects that presidents have sought, according to multiple models and significance tests.

This research on the effect of presidential rhetoric has made a contribution to the field of presidential rhetoric studies. The findings in this book question the outcomes in the analysis of Wood (2007) wherein he states that the "debate should now end over whether presidents' words matter [and] future research should turn to other important questions relating to presidential rhetoric and public opinion" (p. 168). The definitiveness of his statement about the power and the effectiveness of presidential rhetoric must be questioned further. This debate within the field of presidential studies should continue as scholarship attempts to better understand the president's use of the "bully pulpit" to influence externalities.

Considering the findings in this book, it seems that the president's decision to address the economy so often must stem from a symbolic placation or institutional necessity that is intended to comfort constituencies or somehow garner electoral advocacy from the party's base. No other viable explanation really exists given the lack of results presidents obtain from discussing the economy and, on the other hand, their persistent determination to do so (Edwards, 2003). This discrepancy leads one to believe that presidential rhetoric on the economy is, at best, a tool presidents use to appear concerned about the economy and to present the facade, to their constituents, that they are in control of an important facet of American life, the state of the country's economy. Moreover, the economy is essential to presidential success with Congress, reelections, and historical legacy. The truth is that we need a strong economy to maintain our democracy; not many would deny this reality. Thus, presidents naturally want to present themselves as participants in the perpetuation of American democracy because if they fail to do so, they risk being judged harshly by the public and, more importantly, by history.

Chapter Outline

The introduction explicates the theoretical framework underpinning the analysis. The extant arguments about presidents shaping economic outcomes have shown that presidents have influence with economic actors (Eshbaugh-Soha, 2006; Wood, 2004; 2007). Moreover, the research definitively claims that the question regarding presidential influence and power to persuade is undeniable, to the extent that future research should move beyond the question (Wood, 2007). Such a contention is noteworthy. However, it necessitates further inquiry. This is to say nothing of their scholarly work, which is highly respected and offers a serious contribution to the conversation. But, it is one aspect of the relationship between presidential rhetoric and the economy. Nevertheless, I think that assessing how presidential rhetoric shapes the actions of economic actors and presidential economic leadership, with different variables, datasets, and theoretical underpinnings, might offer further insight into the definitiveness of Wood's (2007) assertion. Similar, but theoretically expanded, analyses will help construct a more comprehensive framework for assessing the president's ability to shape the economy, particularly how and to what extent the president can influence the behavior and decisions of these actors; this should facilitate in a determination of presidential influence with those actors who can affect economic indicators.

The discussion regarding the power and effectiveness of presidential rhetoric is contentious. Empirical research asserts that presidents are served well in their economic goals by using the bully pulpit to carry out their agenda. It is clear that presidents speak about the economy more so than any other issue. Presidents treat their rhetoric as a mechanism of power, a way to persuade others to do what they want. In other words, presidential rhetoric shapes economic policy and outcomes. These claims are theoretically suspect, however, especially when you consider the actions of economic actors, the constraints of the separated system of American government, and the assumptions in the notion that the president's rhetoric can engender political will and overcome a vitriolic political process. Assuming that the president is the most important economic actor in the system there are serious questions that should be considered when asserting that presidential rhetoric has the power to shape the behaviors of economic actors. Actually, these analyses produce findings that require further inquiry about whether a president can frame economic conditions to shape the perceptions and actions of economic actors—the overall purpose of this book.

Changes in Federal Funds Rate (1954–2012)

Presidents persistently attempt to use their rhetoric as a mechanism of influence over salient policies. As the economy has become more salient, presidents have tried to gain a semblance of control over its direction and robustness. Yet, the literature is incomplete regarding whether the *rhetoric* is influential with the most pertinent economic actors, particularly the Fed—an institution with substantial authority and influence over the economy. Assessing whether presidential rhetoric shapes the Fed's economic behavior provides one assessment of rhetoric's effect, expanding what we know with regard to presidential power. Utilizing the economic speeches from Dwight D. Eisenhower through Barack Obama, this chapter questions whether the Fed's behavior modeled what the presidents wanted. The results suggest that it is more likely that the Fed is paying attention to Congress and/or the economic indicators rather than the rhetoric of the president.

Public Perceptions of the Economy (1948–2008)

How individuals behave economically affects the economy considerably, and presidents are aware of how important the public is to the economy. Ironically, the public expects the president to make sure the economy is sound. This makes leading the public difficult for presidents. If the public perceives the economy as "good," they are more likely to behave as such, taking risks and spending more. The president wants to use his rhetoric to mitigate the fear of risk for the public so they will consume and invest. Is the president able to shape with positive economic behavior, the public's perception and its behavior? This question has shaped previous studies and guided our perceptions of presidential power and leadership. However, I offer a different method of assessing the public's response to presidential rhetoric and the ability of the president to lead economically.

Instead of using the Consumer Confidence Index as a measure of how the public perceives the president and responds to the positive rhetoric about the economy, I analyzed the National Election Studies (NES) data from Harry S. Truman through George W. Bush to ascertain how the public thinks about the president and his handling of the economy. Using a different dataset offers results that are contrary to many arguments in the literature, namely, that the president can use positive, optimistic rhetoric to shape how the public perceives their economic conditions (Eshbaugh-Soha, 2006; Wood, 2007; 2012; Wood, Owens, and Durham, 2005). The results suggest that the way the public perceives economic conditions cannot fully be determined by the tone of presidential economic rhetoric. Regardless of presidential attempts to tailor their rhetoric to meet specific needs, they are incredibly unsuccessful, in nearly every way; the public does not change their perceptions about the economy when the president tries to convince them that all is well.

Economic Behavior in the Congress (1946–2008)

Some have argued that the president is the preeminent economic policymaker. Given that he is the figure the public holds most accountable for the state of the economy, his unparalleled role gives him a profound and direct influence over the economy as well as those involved in determining the economy's variability, outcomes, and indicators. In short, economic actors such as Congress look to the president for information, guidance, and leadership; his policy rhetoric provides the direction and guidance that substantially impacts the economy. The president understands this reality and often seeks to mitigate intrusion of others and how they influence the direction of economic policy by shaping their economic actions, particularly Congress. Some have argued that members are waiting for leadership and economic policy direction from the president. The reality, however, is that Congress is capable of creating its own mechanisms of policy control that enable members, who are less informed, to garner policy expertise, thus, bypassing the president's signals. The data indicate that presidential rhetoric is not effective in persuading Congress to take economic actions. According to the results suggested in this analysis, the president is not the most important actor in economic policy. In fact, Congress often restricts the president's legislative policy developments; they are not passively waiting for the president to provide leadership on economic policy. Members are concerned with making their own policy and their own reelection, which often leads them in a different direction, economically, than where the president is trying to lead.

Using the data from the *Policy Agendas Project* and *The American Presidency Project*, from presidents Harry S. Truman through George W. Bush—1948 through 2008, I estimated the relationship between presidential economic rhetoric and congressional economic behavior. Connecting these two data sources offers a unique look into the president's ability to shape the economic behavior of Congress. I was then able to determine if economic rhetoric could predict congressional actions regarding the economy. However, the results suggest that congressional actions on the economy seem to stem from external elements such as existing economic conditions rather than positive or negative presidential economic rhetoric. It is clear that there is a lack of significance in predicting changes in congressional behavior. The data suggest that rhetoric serves, rather, as a mechanism of placation and facade of leadership.

Conclusion

The purpose of this book is to utilize a more comprehensive approach for analyzing the effectiveness of the president's rhetoric and then methodologically measure its effect on the economy. It utilized a theory similar to that of Wood (2007) but expanded the scope of the analysis by using different data sets to assess rhetoric's effect on three specific economic entities: the Fed, the Public, and Congress. Determining presidential influence over the behaviors of economic actors and using different data sources allowed for a more comprehensive research operationalization into the contention that the president's ability to influence economic indicators comes from his bully pulpit and his position as the most important economic actor in the system (Cavalli, 2006; Wood, 2007; Wood, Owens, and Durham, 2005; Zarefsky,

2004). However, despite expanding the potential effect of the president's rhetoric on new actors and different databases, the results indicate that presidents have little direct influence over economic actors, and subsequently the economy—they seem to be a product of their contextual *sitz im leben* rather than an entrepreneur.

Therefore, it is my contention that the debate within the field of presidential studies should continue as scholarship attempts to better understand the president's use of the bully pulpit to influence externalities. Rhetoric scholarship needs to substantially modify its approach to presidential rhetoric if it is to continue as a legitimate conversation within presidential studies. It needs to find a better way of classifying presidential rhetoric or clearly differentiating between the various classifications of rhetoric, such as crisis rhetoric, agenda-setting rhetoric, and symbolic rhetoric, and might perhaps also consider rhetoric as it is classified in other scholarship such as frameworks that appeal to the core beliefs of the audiences (Arthur and Woods, 2013; Boydstun, Glazier, and Phillips, 2013; Boydstun, Glazier, and Pietryka, 2013; Glazier and Boydstun, 2012).

CHAPTER ONE

Presidential Rhetoric and the Economy

Did y'ever think . . . that making a speech on economics is a lot like pissing down your leg? It seems hot to you, but it never does to anyone else.

—Lyndon B. Johnson (Galbraith, 1981)

Expectations

The expectations of the president were drastically different in the beginning of the republic than they are in the modern presidency (Corwin, 1958; Tulis, 1987). The presidency was traditionally an institution that provided constitutional leadership, a statutory position; the president was merely a clerk that administrated. The institution, however, underwent a major change. The president is now chosen by the people, generally, and must mobilize them and communicate with them. Moreover, the individual that wants to be president must persuade the people to choose him as their leader. This typically happens by way of presidential rhetoric. Presidents now are expected to use their rhetoric to foster support, if they want to be successful. Presidential power, according to expectation, is now the power to persuade and/or bargain—so presidents think and act suitably (Neustadt, 1991).[1]

Before this transformation, convincing others to support policy positions or an agenda was not a part of the official functions. These actions are now fundamental to the office of the presidency. To be effective, according to Tulis (1987), presidents have to appeal to large audiences of voters and political actors. Presidents are expected to seek out the favor of the American public (Whitford and Yates, 2009). Presidents now participate in a process of "going public" in order to offer their ideas about policy (Kernell, 2007). It is now a democratic expectation, necessary for the democratic institution of the presidency.

Presidents are constantly trying to meet the expectations of their office. Those expectations are increasing at such a dramatic pace that presidents are hard-pressed to meet them (Light, 1999). This is why they turn to every mechanism their position and institution afford to them (Howell, 2003). Neustadt's (1991) explanation of presidential power and how that power can enable a president to meet the expectations set out for him, whether institutionally or from other political actors, is typically predominant.[2] Neustadt (1991) defines presidential power as personal. The presidency is a constitutionally weak institution and therefore, must obtain its power from the person that occupies the office. Presidential power is personal rather than institutional; the person derives their power from their ability to persuade and bargain with other actors and institutions. More people need favors from the president than from any other person; this gives the president bargaining power. Presidential rhetoric is an extension, or rather a mechanism, of a president's power. The rhetoric is one way that presidents try to assert their power and position over other political actors, the public, and institutions; it is their bully pulpit.

Because America has a system of separated institutions sharing power, presidents must persuade/bargain, not command to accomplish the functions and expectations of their office. The problem, however, as seen by some scholars, consists of the assumption of this presidential power (Edwards, 2003; Light, 1999). If presidential power is the power to persuade, why is there such a lack of evidence that proves the president can persuade (Edwards, 2003)? In fact, through analyses of three of the greatest rhetorical presidents (Lincoln, FDR, Reagan), Edwards (2003) shows that presidents do not/cannot use persuasion as a mechanism of changing the political environment. He argues that *events* are the impetus for changes rather than the attempts of presidential persuasion (Edwards, 2009). In other words, the question of whether presidential power is internally or externally controlled is still a matter of serious debate.

Going Public

"Going public" is an attempt to give the president more legislative power and to help him meet the expectations of his office. This strategy is common practice in modern presidential administrations (Kernell, 2007). This change in political strategy and presidential leadership transpired directly after World War I (Tulis, 1987). Going public is in direct contradiction to bargaining; it eradicates the "kinds of exchanges . . . for the American political system to function properly" (Kernell, 2007, p. 3). There is rarely room for compromise. More importantly, however, when a president goes public with a policy request, he keeps Congress from receiving credit; it imposes all negative political costs upon those that do not do what the president requests (Kernell, 2007). This creates direct opposition to the president's requests and produces a contentious environment wherein the president gets less than he wants (Canes-Wrone, 2001; Kernell, 2007).

Kernell's (2007) theory maintains that for the going public strategy to work, presidents need high levels of public approval. In order to accomplish this, presidents have increased many activities that enable them to go public with their messages. For instance, even though major presidential addresses have maintained an equilibrium over the years, minor presidential addresses have increased since President Dwight D. Eisenhower. In addition, public appearances of presidents have steadily increased since President Harry S. Truman. The yearly average for President Franklin D. Roosevelt was about five public appearances, which was common for those presidents who came before him (King and Ragsdale, 1988). To give some perspective, presidents George H. W. Bush and William J. Clinton averaged about 150 public appearances each year. Most of these appearances, however, are accompanied by a speech or remarks of some kind (Kernell, 2007).

The problem, however, is that the audiences for presidential speeches have significantly declined over the years. For example, in 1969, the average households with televisions that viewed presidential speeches were about 50 percent. That number has dwindled to slightly fewer than 30 percent in 2006. Moreover, those watching the State of the Union Address have gone from 60 to 75 percent in 1981 to about 25 to 40 percent in 2006. This is a serious concern for presidents who use going public as a governing strategy (Kernell, 2007).

Approval Ratings[3]

Brace and Hinckley (1992) suggest that the president's ability to manipulate public opinion is highly limited; this is profoundly important for understanding how the president's capacity for meeting expectations is decreasing. They talk about Kernell's (2007) *Going Public* argument and say that presidents do this because of the declining party mechanisms. The president cannot form coalitions with Congress any longer. This may have been so in years past, but it is too difficult now, so presidents take their issues public and try to mobilize public opinion.

The problem, however, is that there is always an inevitable decline of public approval that every president experiences. A coalition of minorities gets upset and decreases their support; this is more pronounced in the second term of any president. In the second term, their approval ratings decline much more quickly than in the first.[4] Such externalities like the economy, crisis, use of force with major address can boost a president's approval ratings for a short term. The public expectations have been growing; the president has been promising more, even overpromising in order to resonate with the public in hopes and anticipation of higher approval numbers (Brace and Hinckley, 1992).[5]

More importantly, however, is their observation that popular presidents win more victories legislatively, but they generally ask for less legislation (Brace and Hinckley, 1992). The higher their public approval ratings are the more they get done in Congress. Also, success in Congress means they get higher approval ratings; it is cyclical. The larger the legislative program and the more positions a president takes, the lower his approval ratings. The importance of this cannot be overstated for the expectations of his office. It shows, undoubtedly, that the public wants him to accomplish legislation, but that they do not want him to do too much. He has to win in order to win, but if he wins too much, he loses. This reality completely affects his ability to meet expectations and how his ability to meet those expectations is diminishing with every win and loss.

The President and the Economy

Despite the gaps in empirical research about the length of time rhetorical influence lasts after speeches, the lack of comprehensive assessments of presidential administrations, and the narrow focus on policy issues, the literature does indicate that presidents are able to influence congressional and public agendas with rhetoric (Lawrence, 2004). Most important, however, is the fact that scholarship has not done much to ascertain how presidential rhetoric influences the subject of what presidents are discussing in their speeches (Eshbaugh-Soha and Peake, 2008; Hanson, 2004; Kalb, Peters, and Woolley, 2006; Tackach, 2002). Therefore, how does presidential rhetoric influence the economy and economic conditions?

The public expects the government to keep the economy improving (Dolan, Frendreis, and Tatalovich, 2008). Despite particular events of national importance, the public regards the economy, specifically, unemployment and inflation, as the number one issue on their minds. This is important to the public; they have substantively linked the president and the economy together. Presidents often lose congressional seats and reelection in the event of an economic downturn (Dolan, Frendreis, and Tatalovich, 2008). Therefore, the president has to be a good manager of the economic responsibilities given to him. He must be able to differentiate between the tools of economic policy: fiscal, monetary, and regulatory policies, which are essential to his role and his ability to shape either (Dolan, Frendreis, and Tatalovich, 2008).

Presidential Economic Policy

The differences between the president's roles in the economy are essential to his ability to influence it (Dolan, Frendreis, and Tatalovich, 2008). There are typically three policy tools he uses to influence the economy: fiscal, monetary, and regulatory. Fiscal policy addresses the spending and taxing elements of the economy for which the government is in charge; this is crucial for economic policymaking. The levels of taxation and government spending are critical for the important economic indicators such as unemployment and inflation. As Dolan, Frendreis, and Tatalovich (2008) explain, the federal government has sought to influence the economy and manipulate its health by making changes to those economic indicators it can change, particularly taxing and spending. Monetary policy, however, is not under the federal government's purview per se (Dolan, Frendreis, and Tatalovich, 2008).

The Federal Reserve (Fed) Board mostly controls it; the president appoints its members. The Fed controls the supply of money and other mechanisms of influence over banks and financial institutions. This element of influence, however, is limited, which I discuss in a later chapter. Presidents, generally, are not able to influence monetary policy as much as fiscal policy (Edwards and Wayne, 1985). The Fed is independent and not subject to the same accountabilities as other bureaucratic agencies. Finally, regulatory policy is a broad stroke of mechanisms used by various government agencies to control the outcomes and indicators of/within the economy (Dolan, Frendreis, and Tatalovich, 2008). There are two essential purposes of regulatory policy, despite all the controversy and differing opinions of its efficiency and effectiveness. The first consists of making conditions favorable for the marketplace to work. The second has to do with keeping social outcomes that negatively impact the market from transpiring (Dolan, Frendreis, and Tatalovich, 2008).

Institutional Changes

Prior to 1929, however, the president's role in the economy was limited by institutional constraints, mainly the Budget and Accountability Act of 1921. This act established the Bureau of the Budget and a system for preparing and submitting to Congress a budget for the entire federal government. After the Great Depression, an institutional role for the president's actions on behalf of the economy became formalized by legislation and by public expectations (Edwards and Wayne, 1985). This role transpired through the enactment of the Employment Act of 1946, which gave the president the responsibility of participating in the creation of a macroeconomic policy for the U.S. government. Presidents now had to submit to Congress an economic plan ten days after submission of the budget. Included in the report was an economic prognosis for the year that covered employment, production, and purchasing power of the United States (Edwards and Wayne, 1985). In 1978, Congress furthered the president's role in reinforcing the economy by enacting the Humphrey-Hawkins Full Employment Act. This legislation also created a unique institutional role for the president in the economy by requiring the president to set standards for monetary policy, inflation, and unemployment rates. Presidents have mostly ignored this piece of legislation by refusing to articulate specific numbers and benchmarks (Wood, 2004).[6]

The increasing pressures and responsibilities of presidential oversight for the economy have forced the president to devote more time and resources to the economy (Edwards and Wayne, 1985). Moreover, presidents have increased their promises about what they will accomplish economically (Dolan, Frendreis, and Tatalovich, 2008). This has compelled presidents to increase their staff and institutional support for economic policymaking, particularly after the Great Depression (Frendreis and Tatalovich, 1994).

Wood (2007) provides a concise summary of the different presidential approaches to economic policy starting with Truman. He states that Truman and Eisenhower only had one policy advisor for the economy, a chairman of the Council for Economic Advisors. This trend changed with Kennedy and Johnson, who funneled advice to the president from the Council of Economic Advisors, Treasury Department, and the Bureau of the Budget (Wood, 2004). Finally, there was some form of economic advisory process from Nixon's centralized Bureau of the Budget to Clinton's perdurable National Economic Council by Executive Order (Stein, 1994).

Given the institutional requirements and mandates, as well as the public's expectations of the president's role in the economy, the president has to factor the economy into his agenda and attend to the needs of the economy (Hoffman and Howard, 2010). In fact, the president will promote the economic philosophies or approaches to problems that he knows he can fix over those of a specific party (Dolan, Frendreis, and Tatalovich, 2008). Doing what is politically viable is his best economic strategy (Edwards and Wayne, 1985).

Public Expectations

The public expects the economy to do well; when the economy does not do well, the public typically holds the president accountable for this, whether through approval ratings, midterm elections, and/or his reelection. The public expectations about the economy are tied to their expectations for the future (Cohen and Hamman, 2003). If the public thinks that the economy is getting worse, their expectations for the future become more grim, which makes the president's job of leading the public more difficult. When the economy is doing poorly, presidents are not typically reelected to office and their approval ratings suffer (Abramowitz, 2008; Beck, 2009; Edwards and Wayne, 1985; Wood, 2004). The Gallup Poll of presidential approval ratings can be correlated to economic performance (Wood, 2007). When the economy is doing well, Americans say that the president is doing his job well. The inverse is also true; when the economy is doing poorly, Americans say that the president is doing his job poorly.

Because of this, presidents address the economy more often (Wood, Owens, and Durham, 2005). Just how often presidents mention the economy varies over time (Wood, 2007). For instance, presidents Truman, Eisenhower, Johnson, and Nixon did not discuss the economy as much as presidents Kennedy, Ford, Carter, Reagan, and George H. W. Bush. According to Wood, Owens, and Durham (2005), the difference in the number of times the economy is mentioned is not statistically significant from the average. However, presidents Clinton and George W. Bush have greatly emphasized the economy in their rhetoric. The data for Obama's presidency are not complete; however, at the time of this project, he had mentioned the economy in nearly 41 percent of all the speeches he had given.[7]

Presidential Economic Rhetoric

Presidents typically do whatever is within their power to set the economic policy agenda, which includes sending positive and negative signals to pertinent political economic actors; presidential speeches are the president's way of conveying his policy preferences to the actors (Eshbaugh-Soha, 2006; Eshbaugh-Soha and Peake, 2005). The speeches send necessary signals about what the president wants; these signals motivate the economic players to action, if and when they are exposed to the rhetoric (Eshbaugh-Soha, 2006). Presidential speeches are mechanisms of power, instruments of the modern presidency that facilitate the president's ability to get what he wants (Eshbaugh-Soha, 2006). If presidents did not think that their economic speeches would bring about their desired results for the economy, they would expend their energy in more productive, behind-the-scenes constituency building.

The expectation from the American public is that the president will lead the economy, particularly through downturns and prosperity (Wood, 2004). This position enables the promotion of policy preferences to economic actors; presidents send signals to economic groups and policymakers about how their actions will be recompensed (Eshbaugh-Soha, 2005). Presidents are able to accomplish this through the submission of the budget, proposed legislation, and issue attention as well as through political appointments.

Many assume that the president would talk more about the economy during times of economic expansion in order to receive credit for the growth. Moreover, one would assume that presidents would discuss a failing economy in terms of how they are going to fix the situation. Presidential rhetoric on the economy, however, does not take into account the macroeconomic conditions (Wood, 2004). A president's rhetoric is consistently present when the economy is doing well and when the economy is doing poorly. This is just as true when presidents talk about unemployment; they are just as likely to discuss unemployment when rates are high as when they are low (Wood, 2004). Presidents are more likely to talk about inflation when rates are high and do not really discuss inflation when rates are low (Wood, 2004). Moreover, when considering the deficit as a portion of the gross domestic product (GDP), presidents are readily paying attention and adjust their rhetoric accordingly (Wood, 2004). For instance, a 1 percent increase in the deficit creates five more instances during that month wherein the president mentions the GDP (Wood, 2004).

How presidents discuss the economy is just as pertinent as when they discuss the economy. The tone of presidential rhetoric depends on the economic conditions during the speech (Wood, 2004). For instance, presidents Truman through Carter were drastically more pessimistic about the economy. Reagan and Bush I were slightly more positive, and Clinton was dramatically positive about the economy (Wood, 2007). Bush II altered the upward trend and became more negative when discussing the economy. President Obama, so far, offered a balance of negative rhetoric and optimistic rhetoric, depending upon the audience.

Presidents Truman through Bush II (first term), economic growth and unemployment did not affect the general tone of presidential rhetoric (Wood,

2004). When considering the deficit and inflation, however, the tone and optimism change in significant ways. When inflation goes up, the rhetoric of optimism goes down, and, when the deficit goes down, the optimistic rhetoric increases significantly (Wood, 2004). Presidential rhetoric regarding the economy has become increasingly optimistic over time despite the differences in administrations and economic conditions (Wood, 2004).

Presidents have not addressed the economy in a major way in five of the last eleven recessions. In fact, presidents speak more about noneconomic-related issues during a recession than economic issues (Hoffman and Howard, 2010). Presidents offer fewer speeches during times of recession, inflation, and low employment (Ragsdale, 1987). There is a reason for this: constructing too dramatic a picture of the economy can have seriously negative effects. Moreover, presenting the economy as better than it actually is or ignoring the realities makes the president seem out of touch or incompetent, both of which can affect his interaction with important political actors or the electorate (Hoffman and Howard, 2010). They rarely, if ever, make major economic speeches to inform the public how well the economy is doing.

Presidents decrease their policy speeches when the economy is doing poorly (Eshbaugh-Soha, 2010b). In fact, presidents tend to ignore the worsening economic conditions rather than addressing them. This is a change from times past, wherein presidents used to react strongly to worsening economic conditions. Presidents do this to avoid drawing the media's attention to the bad economic conditions, over which they have limited influence. Presidents have a hard enough time controlling what the media covers in a good economy; it is worse with the negative economy (Eshbaugh-Soha and Peake, 2005).

Direct Influence of Presidential Rhetoric on the Economy

Signaling theory and impact assessment methodology suggest that presidential signals, consistent speeches about the state of the economy and the president's policy plans for the economy, inform the market of the president's positions and economic goals, which affect the market (Eshbaugh-Soha, 2005). Extant research suggests that the consistent, substantive, and symbolic messages in the president's economic speeches provide the necessary conditions that allow the president to affect the economy directly. Accordingly, should the optimism of presidential speeches affect the public perception of the economy, which is seen in how consumers perceive economic news and the consumer's attitude toward the economy (Wood, Owens, and Durham, 2005)? Can presidential speeches addressing the economy alter consumer behavior in terms of risks and spending?[8] Are presidents able to use their rhetoric to influence the confidence of economic actors? Using signals that consumers absorb, is the president able to influence the most important economic actors? Does the optimism in the speeches filter through the economic actors and consumers back into the economy, creating a consistent message that can "establish a climate for economic perceptions" (Wood, 2007, p. 14)? Is this climate something that the president can then manipulate to his advantage?

Measuring the spending, borrowing, and investing of consumers and businesses shows rhetoric's effect statistically. The personal consumption data and business data from the Federal Reserve Bank from 1981 through 2005 show the economic actors and their perceptions about the strength of the economy (Wood, 2007). The prevailing theory suggests that consumers take cues from the president about their economic futures. The argument is, if he is positive about the economy in his speeches, then consumers respond accordingly, thus reinforcing positive outcomes in the economic indicators. Using vector autoregression (VAR) and Grangers causal relationships, Wood (2007) produces results that show that presidential optimism in rhetoric affects personal consumption and business investment.

His research shows that the optimism in presidential speeches about the economy was able to influence consumer confidence, which affected various elements of macroeconomic performance (Wood, Owens, and Durham, 2005). He argues that individual choices affect macroeconomic performance for aggregate economic outcomes, because two-thirds of all U.S. economic activity is driven by personal consumption. He maintains that how individuals behave economically affects the economy considerably (Wood, Owens, and Durham, 2005). When consumers decided not to spend, there are drastic and lasting reactions. For instance, limited consumer consumption can lead to unemployment, and liberal spending can lead to inflation, neither of which is particularly good for the economy. He suggests that consumers take cues from the president about their economic future. Thus, the theory states that if the president is positive about the economy in his speeches, then consumers respond accordingly, reinforcing the positive outcomes in the economic indicators, particularly economic growth (Wood, Owens, and Durham, 2005).

Presidential Rhetoric's Limited Influence on the Economy

Presidents do not have the ability to simply change the inflation rate or the unemployment rate or any other economic indicator. These indicators are outside of their institutional and statutory authority. For instance, the Clinton administration's signals to the bond market did not make a significant difference; there was no effect on the Thirty-Year Treasury Bills despite the rhetoric (Eshbaugh-Soha, 2005). President George H. W. Bush's signals to the market about the money supply in his State of the Union Addresses were not effective. In fact, his signals returned the opposite outcomes. Such data and results suggest that the president has a limited influence over monetary policy (Eshbaugh-Soha, 2005). Moreover, studies show that in the pre-golden (1953–1962), golden (1963–1985), and the post-golden (1986–2002) age television eras, presidential rhetoric had no significant effect on how the public viewed economic policy (Young and Perkins, 2005). Some research suggests that the presidents, through their rhetorical actions, are limited in their ability to influence economic effects or economic indicators directly (Rockman, 1984).

Coda

The empirical research on presidential rhetoric is becoming more comprehensive and rooted in theory. This research argues that presidential rhetoric is important and that it matters what presidents say. For instance, Wood (2007) states that the "debate should now end over whether presidents' words matter . . . future research should turn to other important questions relating to presidential rhetoric and public opinion" (p. 168). However, a comprehensive and consistent argument of how the limitations presented by institutions and the political process influence presidential rhetoric has not been built completely. The theories and data usage in the literature about the president's direct affect on the economy are weak and incomplete (Eshbaugh-Soha, 2005). The literature seems to ignore the limitations pressing against the argument that substantive effects can be obtained by rhetoric. Creating an analysis that contributes to the construction of a larger, workable scholarly literature on the limitations of presidential rhetoric's ability to produce substantive effects in the economy enhances the current literature.

Notes

1. Scholarship has been focused upon determining whether rhetoric produces the effects the presidents seek. The literature reveals that how the analysis of rhetoric is conducted is crucial to understanding if rhetoric actually produces those desired effects. There is a major difference between assessing the effect of individual speeches and that of aggregated speeches infused with cues and signals to elite policymakers. Rhetorical strategies in individual, televised speeches are not worth the invested time and amounts of energy presidents expend; according to the data, the speeches do not offer positive returns for presidents (Edwards, 2003). The rhetoric does not

institute the policy effects desired (Edwards and Wood, 1999). The president cannot move audiences toward what he wants with rhetoric in any form. Therefore, no change transpires from the hearing of an individual presidential speech (Edwards, 1983). The literature has mostly accepted what Edwards (2003) argued and it responded by producing research that asserts presidential rhetoric's effect can be seen in the analysis of *aggregated* speeches, those speeches that were infused with signals and cues to elite policymakers. Research now analyzes presidential rhetoric by aggregated speeches and cue/signaling methodologies. This research seeks to address whether the president's use of aggregated rhetoric and cues/signals can influence programs, positions, and policies. The claim is that the consistent, substantive, and symbolic messages in the president's speeches provide the necessary conditions that allow the president to affect the content of the speech directly (Eshbaugh-Soha, 2006; Wood, 2007). The speeches, when aggregated and infused with cues/signals, can create responses and attention that major, individual, televised speeches cannot accomplish. However, this approach is in its infancy, and the effectiveness of such a strategy is yet to be determined (Edwards, 2003).

2. Neustadt (1991) maintains that there are rare instances wherein the president's words are taken as actions; he does not command anyone unless these five elements are present. The first is that the request or command is completely unambiguous. There has to be assurance that the president has spoken or commanded that something be done. Secondly, there has to be complete clarity of meaning. Thirdly, the public has to be aware of what the president wants. The command has to be publicized. Fourthly, there has to exist an ability to carry out what was said or asked by the president. Lastly, there has to exist a perception of authority; there has to exist an understanding that what the president wants done is his right to have done. When these are present, it is as though the words are action. The president's professional reputation enables him to bargain successfully (Neustadt, 1991). The "Washingtonians" have to think that he is an effective politician. He has to press the advantages and mitigate the disadvantages. He has to create, in the Washingtonians, a mindset that if they cross him, there is a major price to pay; there are consequences for not doing what the president wants. They have to know if he can be pushed around. If he can be, they will not think highly of his professional reputation. If there is a pattern emerging of him letting them down, this will damage his professional reputation. Secondly, the president has to have public prestige to bargain successfully; he must have support outside of Washington (Neustadt, 1991). This is a case wherein presidents anticipate the reactions of the voters. The president must watch Congress and how they judge the mood of the public toward the president. The perception of a "low prestige" conveys a message that it is ok to resist the president. Such an action limits his bargaining power. Therefore, he has to think proscriptively about his choices and how he manages the public (Neustadt, 1991). The president must take measures to protect his power. Choices are the building blocks of success (Neustadt, 1991). Every choice that the president makes is laden with power prospects. He has to decide how each choice will affect his power and resources. Neustadt (1991) im-

plies that a president should never make a decision that will deplete or diminish his power; power comes to those who sense of what power is made. Only the president can see the issue the way it impacts his future power prospects. He does this through his self-image of confidence and a sense of direction. He cannot let others make decisions that affect his power. Only this allows him to understand the implications of that power. Knowing what power is, having a good professional reputation and public prestige, and knowing how to bargain will definitely help or paralyze a president's attempt to accomplish the expectations of his office.

3. Page, Shapiro, and Dempsey (1987) and Page and Shapiro (1992) cover a range of fifty years of presidential rhetoric; their research suggests that rhetoric had an effect on policy preferences when the president possessed approval ratings of 50 percent or higher.

4. President Clinton is the exception to this argument. Brace and Hinckley (1992) maintain that this anomaly is because of the economy.

5. They maintain that what would help the president would be to keep the standards for support to the numbers that he obtained in the election. They say that the standards for popularity need to change. Citizens could expect presidents to behave more like statesmen instead of politicians if this changed. It might force changes in their behavior. The increasing attention to poll numbers has changed the dynamics of democratic accountability. Presidents used to have four years before they were evaluated, now they are evaluated monthly and it is a highly fickle process. Presidential approval should be based only on those persons who voted for the president; this would eliminate the downfalls of the "Public Relations Presidency."

6. See Wood (2004) and Frendreis and Tatalovich (1994) for a discussion of how presidents have mostly ignored this legislation's mandates.

7. 1,677 out of 4,121 speeches mentioned the economy. This data is from January 20, 2009, to December 4, 2012.

8. Presidential "saber rattling" affects economic indicators and perceptions of those indicators (Wood, 2009; 2012). The constant discussion of war, Americans in harm's way, and conflict with other countries produces seriously negative outcomes for economic performance.

CHAPTER TWO

Ascertaining Presidential Influence with Economic Actors

> How does a public leader find just the right word or the right way to say no more and no less than he means to say? Bearing in mind that anything he says may topple governments and may involve the lives of innocent men? How does that leader speak the right phrase, in the right way, under the right conditions, to suit the accuracies and contingencies of the moment when he is discussing questions of policy, so that he does not stir a thousand misinterpretations and leave the wrong connotation or impression? How does he reach the immediate audience and how does he communicate with the millions of others who are out there listening from afar? The President, who must call his people and summon them to meet their responsibilities as citizens, . . . often ponders these questions and searches for the right course.
>
> —Lyndon B. Johnson (Woolley and Peters, 2014—"Lyndon B. Johnson, 1968")

The President's Connection to the Economy

Those who argue that the president *does* have a direct connection to the economy fail to consider the subtleties of what transpires between the incidents of presidential rhetoric and the actions that substantiate the changes in the economy, the constraints of the separated system of American government, and the limitations of the president's ability to use rhetoric to achieve desired results (Edwards, 2003). Conversely, those who maintain that the president does *not* have a direct connection to the economy neglect to consider the influence of the following: the consistency and prevalence of aggregated speeches about the state of the economy, the president's institutional and legal mandates concerning the economy, and the president's policy plans for the economy on said economic indicators/conditions (Eshbaugh-Soha, 2005; Wood, 2007). Because of these divergent views, this matter should be addressed, particularly given the amount of time presidents spend talking about the economy, the influence the government and the economy have on one another, and the important role the economy plays in political affairs.

I am, however, cautious about accepting the claim in the literature that the direct influence presidents have on the Consumer Confidence Sentiment Index definitely answers whether presidential economic rhetoric matters to the extent that research should move beyond the question (Wood, 2007). I think that one cannot simply assess an "optimistic outlook" in the president's rhetoric on a limited list of economic indicators and claim that presidential tone can make the economy, indirectly, better or worse with such conviction (Eshbaugh-Soha, 2006; Wood, 2007). The results of Wood's (2007) highly respected analysis are only one aspect of the relationship between presidential rhetoric and the economy. I am skeptical of this approach because the presidents do not have any authority over, or legal connection to, those indicators. Moreover, they struggle with obtaining a consistent audience and are limited in their coalition building endeavors.

Therefore, a more comprehensive framework for an analysis of the president's influence over the economy should determine the type of connection and influence presidents have over the most important economic actors, who can bring change to economic indicators, instead of assuming that the presidents are the most important economic actor in the system (Wood, 2007; Wood, Owens, and Durham, 2005). I think that assessing the research question further, with different variables, datasets, and theoretical underpinnings, might offer further insight into the definitiveness of Wood's (2007) assertion. Similar, but theoretically expanded, analyses will help construct a more comprehensive framework for assessing the president's ability to shape the economy, particularly how and to what extent the president can influence the behavior and decisions of these actors; this should facilitate in a determination of presidential influence with those actors who can affect economic indicators. Ascertaining how and if the president can influence these actors to alter their behavior with regard to the economy provides a research operationalization that shows a more comprehensive assessment of how and if the presidential rhetoric matters so influentially (Cavalli, 2006; Zarefsky, 2004). If the tone of presidential rhetoric can predict changes in the behaviors of economic actors, then one could more confidently state that presidents have or do not have a direct influence over the economy.

Theoretical Framework

For the president to have a direct influence on the economy, certain conditions have to exist. The presidents rely on their speeches, written documents, and traveling schedules to get their messages across. Moreover, presidents utilize the "economic sub-presidency" to provide the various economic actors with economic messages (Anderson, 1993, p. 249). The president needs the most important economic actors to which he is connected to pay attention to his rhetoric and act accordingly. It is, however, important to note that, assuming that the president does reach these actors, the actors have to accept that what the president wants is, in fact, what they want for themselves—there can be no differences in agenda or expected outcomes. The president's requests have to be completely unambiguous (Neustadt, 1991). There has to be assurance that the president has spoken or signaled that he wants something to be done a specific way or expects a specific outcome. This is the challenge: signaling the appropriate audience for the appropriate economic action. Moreover, those to whom the president is signaling or speaking must have an ability to carry out what the president desires. Therefore, the most appropriate economic actors that are signaled consist of the Federal Reserve (Fed), the public, and Congress.

The Fed, an independent agency that deals with policies and procedures that influence the economy, is charged with regulating and participating in economic actions, particularly monetary policy. Presidents must use their rhetoric to cue or signal the Fed to bring the agency in line with presidential desires for the economy. For this to occur, presidents have to convince them to take actions that will create changes in the Federal Funds Rate (FFR) (Dolan, Frendreis, and Tatalovich, 2008). The Fed can make the money it loans expensive (raising interest rates) or cheap (lowering interest rates), which has a significant influence with the overall health of the economy.

Secondly, the public plays a vital role in the economy and in the decisions of the president. It is essential that the president have the support of the public in order to accomplish anything with regard to the economy. They have to listen to his rhetoric and agree with how he is handling the economy; members of the public have to think that what the president wants for the economy is what they want for the economy. If the president is able to accomplish this state of agreement, two events also have to transpire. The first is that the people have to believe that the economy is strong so that they are more likely to spend money and thus reinforce the robust economy. They have to think that it is acceptable to engage in economic risks, such as investing, spending, and loaning as well as buying and trading. The second element consists of the people responding to the president's rhetoric with such conviction about the strength of the economy, based upon what the presidents have said, that they are willing to participate in some sort of advocacy on his behalf—this is to say nothing of whether or not said advocacy works.

Lastly, Congress has to be able to accept what the presidents say about the economy as truthful, particularly that the economy is doing well or getting better from a previous economic downturn or that the economy will get worse without the implementation of the proposed policies from the president. Presidential rhetoric has to convince Congress that it is acceptable to alter or maintain existing economic policies, such as taxing and spending. And, they have to convince Congress that what they want Congress to enact is sellable to its constituents. Congress has to be convinced that the presidents are taking the country in the direction that it and its constituents want the economy to go, particularly in terms of policy. In fact, the presidents have to create, in the "Washingtonians," a mindset that, if they disagree with the president, there is a major price to pay (Neustadt, 1991).

For the president to have a direct effect upon economic indicators he needs to garner an acceptable response from each of the aforementioned economic actors; to assume that all of these conditions would happen is suspect and engenders a profound skepticism regarding one's understanding of the political process. Even if all of the conditions[1] explicated by Neustadt (1991) exist when the president is discussing the economy, the argument that presidential rhetoric influences the economy fails to consider the possibility that the economic actors are not listening or have agendas of their own (Edwards, 2003; Fenno, 1978; Jacobs and Shapiro, 2000; Smith and Deering, 1990). The argument assumes that economic actors are waiting to hear from the president about what economic decisions they should make or, even more far-fetched, that they can be persuaded to change their minds about how they had previously decided to act rather than acknowledging that they rarely if ever listen to and agree with the president (Edwards, 1983; 2003; Krehbiel, 1991; Light, 1999; Lowi, 1985).

Moreover, the assertion does not take into consideration that there are external controls imposing on the goals of the presidents, such as resources, political capital, and public approval as well as electoral margin and reputation (Light, 1999). In fact, all of the president's resources are incredibly scarce; resources are essential to presidential agendas, but yet they begin to decline immediately upon assuming the presidency, leaving the presidents less effective and less influential with regard to the economic actors (Light, 1999). Therefore, I argue that the circumstances needed for presidents to affect the economy through rhetoric are not likely to happen because of the externalities involved in the political process, externalities over which the president has little control.

For instance, the president's ability to motivate the Fed to make monetary policy decisions that benefit the president is complicated (Brehm and Gates, 1997). Such policy decisions are not controlled by presidents, but are controlled inside the Fed. Historically, there is a desire for presidents to influence this agency and the various economic actors it employs; however, this is usually not very effective. The discretion by the Fed, where their localities lie, and to whom they are accountable are all factors that keep the decisions within the organization and away from the presidents.

The decisions that the Fed makes can sabotage or undermine the policy goals of the presidents (Brehm and Gates, 1997). In addition, the structure of the relationship allows the Fed to achieve their own goals, which are purely self-interested (Downs, 1967). This means that the requests that come from the president are not precisely what will be pursued and implemented at the Fed. The president's influence is even further complicated by the fact that the Fed is an independent bureaucratic agency.[2] Moreover, even though it features a seven-member board of governors, appointed by the president, there is no guarantee that the appointees will remain loyal to the policies of the president (Edwards and Wayne, 1985). Many appointees in bureaucratic agencies "go native" once they are immersed in the agency culture and begin advocating for the plans of the agency rather than those of the president who appointed them (DiClerico, 2000).

Using cues and signals, presidents offer their ideas about economic policy to the public as a way to garner support; it is a mechanism that presidents think will enable them to circumvent Congress (Kernell, 2007). More importantly, however, when a president "goes public" with a policy request, he keeps Congress from receiving credit for or the benefits of doing what is required. This imposes all of the negative political costs upon those who do not do what the president requests (Kernell, 2007). This can, in fact, create direct opposition to the president's requests and create a contentious environment wherein the presidents are unsuccessful legislatively (Kernell, 2007; Canes-Wrone, 2001). The consequences of this strategy (a breakdown in the political bargaining necessary for policy development) are that the presidents have to appeal more and more to the public because other political actors will not bargain with them (Kernell, 2007; Neustadt, 1991).

The cues and signals that presidents use struggle to shape the public's perceptions of the economy. Moreover, there is no substantial empirical evidence that indicates presidents have influenced them to make changes in behavior (Edwards, 2003; Krause, 1994). There is no systematic study that suggests that the president is able to accomplish what he wants by "going public" (Barrett, 2004; 2005). In many cases, the majority of the people cannot remember a single point the president has discussed in any given speech (Edwards, 2003, p. 208). Therefore, presidents are not able to move the perceptions of the public from unfavorable to favorable with regard to the direction of economic policy. For instance, in the Gallup's "Most Important Problem" list, the economy or an economic issue such as unemployment tops the chart nearly every year since 1936, which questions the president's ability to convince the public that the economy is doing well or getting better (Dolan, Frendreis, and Tatalovich, 2008).

Presidents have increasingly endeavored to influence Congress, particularly with cues and signals; whether or not the influence is substantial in economic policy is debatable. Congress has goals that may be different from or even contrary to those of the president; there is congressional competition for agenda space (Light, 1999). The Congress and possibly each of its members may have more important goals to which their constituents want them to attend. In fact, some members, particularly those of the opposing party, may have a primary goal of obstructing the president's objectives for the economy. Moreover, the major political parties are a weakened institution; the tension has increased to the point where "bipartisanship" is a liability for political actors. This makes it difficult for presidents to build coalitions, which are necessary to accomplish any passage of legislation.

Therefore, this analysis contributes to the literature by pointing out the limitations of the president's ability to use rhetoric to influence economic actors to take actions that would benefit the president. This objective is accomplished by analyzing the president's public speeches on the economy, how the audiences respond to that rhetoric, and the externalities that must be considered when analyzing the effect of presidential rhetoric on the economy. There is no definitive argument in the literature explicating the limitations of presidential rhetoric and its ability to influence others to take actions on the economy (Whitford and Yates, 2009). There is an assumption that what presidents say matters rather than a comprehensive empirical determination of whether such claims can be substantiated. Does the rhetoric engender substantive actions or are the presidents' decisions to address the economy so often a symbolic placation or institutional necessity intended to comfort constituencies or garner electoral advocacy? A comprehensive empirical assessment that helps to obtain the probability that specific control variables will create a change in the behavior of the economic actors as a result of presidential rhetoric will determine if the rhetoric matters in the way that some of the literature suggests.

Rhetorical Classification

Classifying presidential rhetoric identifies the way in which the president expects his rhetoric to work and what he expects from those to whom it was directed (Windt, 1986). I used tone (positivity, negativity, and neutrality) as the primary way of assessing presidential influence. Using tone to determine how rhetoric influences the political process is common in political science literature (Arthur and Woods, 2013; Baumgartner and Jones, 2009; Eshbaugh-Soha, 2006; Wood, 2007). Coding the speeches as "positive" must be differentiated from "optimism" wherein the president talks about what he thinks the economy is going to do in the future, a hopeful plea of the good times that are coming. Positivity, in this analysis, refers specifically to the state of the economy at the time of mention (see table 2.1). This includes any discussion, direct or indirect, that associates the actions of the president with positive economic outcomes, a credit claiming if you will. If the president claims to have moved the economy toward positive economic growth, such as creating jobs for American workers, having better wages, lessening the burden to tax payers, growing real estate values, economic expansion, it was coded as positive. The effect of "good" economic policies that are supported by the presidents and their opposition may be described in clearly positive terms or actions that the president did accomplish (credit claiming), a decision that moved the economy toward growth or kept it from getting worse. Furthermore, this includes the president saying that the economy is doing well because of the type of economic policies he has implemented or for which he is advocating.

Negative coding includes any mention, direct or indirect, that associates the actions of other economic actors with negative economic outcomes or moving the economy away from positive economic growth; this includes mentions such as: taking away jobs from American workers, driving down wages, an added cost to tax payers, hurt real-estate values, or generally "hurts" to the economy (see table 2.2). The effect of "bad" economic policies that are supported by the president's opposition may be described in clearly negative terms or in less offensive ways such as opposing those policies of the president. Furthermore, this includes the president saying that the economy is doing badly because of the opposition he has received for the type of

Table 2.1. Example Sentences Measuring the Positivity of Presidential Economic Rhetoric.

	Speeches from The American Presidency Project
D. D. Eisenhower 1/10/1960	Our economy is strong, expanding, and fundamentally sound.
L. B. Johnson 10/22/1965	We take justifiable pride in our growing national economy and in the ever-higher living standards being achieved by most Americans.
R. M. Nixon 8/15/1971	The tax reductions I am recommending, together with this broad upturn of the economy which has taken place in the first half of this year, will move us strongly forward toward a goal this nation has not reached since 1956, fifteen years ago: prosperity with full employment in peacetime.
J. E. Carter 1/06/1978	Our economy is prosperous and growing . . .
R. W. Reagan 1/11/1986	The economy is in better shape today because we've worked hard to get the federal government out of your pockets and off your backs.
G. H. W. Bush 6/12/1990	And Republicans are the ones who want to keep this economy strong, and we fought every step of the way against those who want to bring America to a grinding halt . . .
W. J. Clinton 1/6/1995	We have grown the private economy as we have cut Government. That's a real recovery and a real bargain for the American people.
G. W. Bush 7/19/2008	Despite the challenges we have faced, our economy has demonstrated remarkable resilience.
B. H. Obama 1/25/2011	We are poised for progress. Two years after the worst recession most of us have ever known, the stock market has come roaring back, corporate profits are up, the economy is growing again.

Adapted from *The American Presidency Project*, 2014.

economic policies he has implemented or for which he is advocating to be implemented. This also includes mentions of the challenges that the American economy faces, whether domestically or internationally.[3]

Parameters of the Analysis

The limitation of this study is that it is not a complete picture of presidential rhetoric on the economy; as such an undertaking would not be feasible. Presidential mentions of the economy and economy-related keywords number in the hundreds of thousands over the entire "rhetorical presidency" (1913–2013). Expecting a researcher to code and operationalize every instance wherein the president signals or cues an economic actor to do

Table 2.2. Example Sentences Measuring the Negativity of Presidential Economic Rhetoric.

	Speeches from The American Presidency Project
D. D. Eisenhower 4/20/1955	Our economy cannot be strong and continue to expand without the development of healthy economic conditions in other free nations, and without a continuous expansion of international trade.
L. B. Johnson 05/18/1965	Improvements in our unemployment compensation system are essential if the program is to exert a stronger stabilizing effect on the economy and provide people with adequate income when out of work. The system has not kept pace with the times.
R. M. Nixon 2/02/1970	The current actions we are taking are designed to help the American economy regain its balance.
J. E. Carter 1/31/1977	Most economists have projected that, without further stimulus, the economy would grow by an inadequate 4.5–5 percent in 1977.
R. W. Reagan 2/18/1981	We can no longer procrastinate and hope that things will get better. They will not. Unless we act forcefully—and now—the economy will get worse.
G. H. W. Bush 10/16/1990	And now we are in a battle in Washington to keep the economy moving forward, to get it revitalized. And the best thing we can do to revitalize it is to get a budget-deficit agreement that gets the deficit down by $500 billion over five years and does it in an enforceable way.
W. J. Clinton 2/17/1993	For more than anything else, our task tonight as Americans is to make our economy thrive again.
G. W. Bush 1/05/2002	We have a war to wage and a recession to fight. Defending our country and strengthening our economy are great priorities for 2002. We must be determined, and we must keep our focus.
B. H. Obama 7/02/2010	The recession dug us a hole of about eight million jobs deep, and we continue to fight headwinds from volatile global markets. So we still have a great deal of work to do to repair the economy and get the American people back to work.

Adapted from *The American Presidency Project*, 2014.

something about the economy is unreasonable.[4] Even using content analysis software would not mitigate the difficulties; one cannot ascertain each word the presidents use to discuss the economy to create a test file (Wood, 2007).[5] For instance, there are words and concepts that affect the economy that deal with trade, gross domestic product, and manufacturing as well as the international balance of payments position, commodities, and numerous other terms that are buried in presidential rhetoric—all too vast to ascertain and, subsequently, code appropriately. Therefore, the significant challenge is in the classification of presidential rhetoric, as mentioned earlier. For this analysis, I chose the tone of the speeches, one aspect of the president's influence, in order to determine how presidential economic rhetoric can motivate economic actors in their economic behavior (Dolan, Frendreis, and Tatalovich, 2008).

In order to reduce the impracticality of analyzing the entire population of presidential mentions of the economy, as other scholars have done, I employed a stratified random sample to obtain an appropriate database of presidential economic rhetoric (Barrett, 2004; Barrett and Eshbaugh-Soha, 2007; Hopkins and King, 2010; Jacobs and Shapiro, 2000; Lohr, 2010; Peterson, 1990; Spriggs, 1996). As illustrated by figure 2.1, for each president, if there were one hundred or fewer speeches, I coded all of them. If there were more than one hundred speeches that met the population, I took 101 speeches from the sample of each presidential administration. Later presidents mentioned the economy more often than earlier presidents. To account for this, I took 10 percent, plus one, of their total speeches if one hundred speeches totaled less than 10 percent of the overall speeches (Lohr, 2010). I conducted the sample in this manner because the population is measured over sixty-five years (1946–2012); this approach will keep the "population drift" from biasing the sample (Hopkins and King, 2010). The language presidents use to discuss the economy changed over time. Thus, taking a random sample of the entire population would have biased the results and discredited the analysis.

I chose to use presidential speeches that included the term "economy" as the population to be studied. The total population consists of 12,775 individual speeches or written documents that mention the term economy from January 1, 1946, through January 19, 2012. These dates fall within the rhetorical presidency, President Harry S. Truman through President Barack H. Obama (Tulis, 1987). This provided me with 1,653 presidential speeches (units of analysis) that mention the term "economy" at least once. I handled more than one mention of the term "economy" in a speech by treating all mentions of the term as one unit of analysis and then, subsequently, coding the term based upon the overall tone of the entire portion of the speech that addressed the economy (Jacobs and Shapiro, 2000). If there were instances wherein two different "tones" could be present, I simply took the tone closest to the beginning of the speech (Woods and Arthur, 2014). This coding decision is justifiable given the research, namely, that presidents struggle to hold their audiences' attention for long periods of time and therefore, discuss the most important agenda items at the beginning of their speeches (Arthur and Woods, 2013; Baum and Kernell, 1999; Edwards, 2003; Eshbaugh-Soha and Peake, 2006; Kernell, 2007; Welch, 2003).

To accommodate each model for each economic actor, I had to code the speeches by day and then aggregate them into other units of analysis:

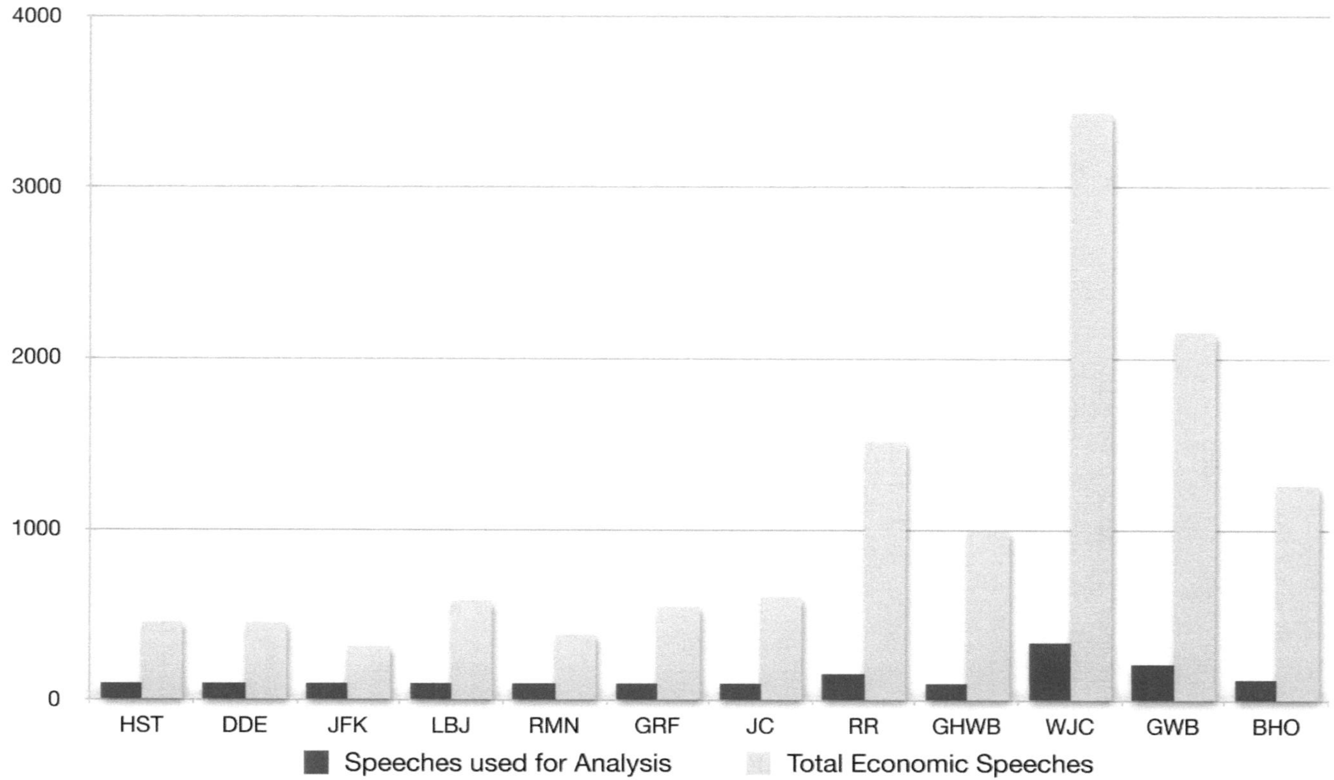

Figure 2.1. Presidential Speeches on the Economy.
Adapted from *The American Presidency Project,* 2014.

month (Fed), four-year election cycle (public), and month (Congress). This provided me with 573 units of analysis for the chapter addressing the Fed, 10,000 units of analysis for the chapter addressing the public, and 610 units of analysis for the chapter addressing Congress. The coding was consistently treated in the same fashion: I coded each mention of the economy in the speech based upon the overall tone of the entire discussion of the portion of the speech that addressed the economy. Essentially, I treated each mention of the term "economy" as one recording unit.

There are multiple instances wherein the presidents mention other economic terms or indicators without the use of the word "economy" in the discussion. For instance, the president may mention "inflation" or "unemployment" and not use the term "economy" in a speech. The initial research and data collection accounted for these terms. I coded their tone as I did with the population economy in the final analysis. I found, however, that there was high correlation between the overall tone of the speech and the tone of the specific economic keywords that presidents use to discuss the economy. I chose to purposefully ignore those instances in order to focus on the population of speeches including the term "economy," a popular buzzword/signal, which still provides an important and significant inquiry into the study of presidential rhetoric.

Independent Variables

I identified the presidential rhetoric aimed at the Fed, the public, and Congress by using the *Public Papers of the President* housed in *The American Presidency Project*'s online database to track presidential speeches by keyword from July 1946 through January 19, 2012.[6] This analysis enabled me to create a document of the compiled speeches wherein the president addresses the economy. As other scholars have done, I decided not to use content analysis software to compile and categorize the language (Arthur and Woods, 2013; Barrett, 2004; 2005; Cameron, 2000). The human coding approach is effective, with intercoder reliability, which I employed (Arthur and Woods, 2013; Wood, 2007; Woods and Arthur, 2014;).

There are pertinent independent variables for each economic actor, the Fed, the public, or the Congress, not all variables are necessary for each actor. However, the foremost mechanism of assessment in each analysis for each economic actor is tone (positivity, negativity); it is a common method of determining how rhetoric influences the political process and institutions in political science literature (Arthur and Woods, 2013; Baumgartner and Jones, 2009; Eshbaugh-Soha, 2006; Wood, 2007). Smith (1983) has argued that not all presidential messages, cues, and/or signals are the same; particularly, there is a difference between the president's intentions for news conferences, town hall meetings, major speeches (televised), interviews, and off-the-cuff remarks with regard to effectiveness and intent. Similarly, even the State of the Union addresses and Executive Orders can vary with regard to the clarity of the presidential message and the feasibility of the presidential request (Eshbaugh-Soha and Peake, 2005). This leads me to question the action of placing them all together, especially if they are each expected, by the presidents, to have a different effect.

Coding Reliability

Testing the reliability of the data was a significant concern. I employed standard intercoder agreement tests on all the variables using roughly 10 percent (160 speeches) of the total economic speeches of President Harry S. Truman through President Barack H. Obama's third year. The coder received only minimal training on how to code the content of presidential speeches according to the codebook and protocol. The coder read 160 presidential speeches, from a random sample, on the economic search terms for the Fed, the public, and Congress and identified the tone, the mechanism of influence frameworks, and the economic frameworks for the discussion of the economy. As presented in table 2.3, the percentages of agreement on the twelve variables ranged from 92.5 percent to 99.4 percent. I also used Scott's pi, which corrects for chance agreement so that the reliability was not obtained by guessing or chance probability. According to Riffe, Lacy, and Fico (2005), this measure is a better method to determine reliability. The results ranged from 0.80 to 0.96 on every variable. Moreover, I used alpha levels of 0.80 or higher as the measure of significant reliability (Krippendorff, 1978).[7]

Table 2.3. Intercoder Reliability Statistics.

	Stratified Random Sample of Presidential Rhetoric N = 160			
	Measures of Reliability		*Measures of Agreements*	
	% Agreement	*Scott's Pi*	*Agreements*	*Disagreements*
Positive Statements	94.4	0.85	151	9
Negative Statements	96.9	0.91	155	5
Neutral Statements	98.8	0.80	158	2

Notes

1. There has to be assurance that the president has spoken or signaled that he wants something to be done. There has to be complete clarity of meaning in what he says. The public has to be aware of what he wants. Those to whom he is signaling have to have an ability to carry out what the president desires. There has to exist an understanding that what he wants to accomplish is his right to have done.

2. Morris (2000) maintains that the Fed is a unique federal bureaucratic agency when compared to the other federal agencies. It does not request a budget from Congress; it is self-sustaining. In fact, the Fed returns billions of dollars every year to the Treasury Department, profit it does not need. This situation provides the Fed with an unparalleled advantage; it does not have to pander to the president.

3. Neutral coding includes any mention, direct or indirect, that does not have negative or positive tones associated with it. The mentions would be general mentions of the term "economy" that are not policy related or addressing the U.S. economy. For example, mentions that say, "a strong and vital economy are important" show the neutrality.

4. Even when considering employing Hopkins and King's (2010) work on *Automated Nonparametric Content Analysis* of blog posts, this undertaking is too complex. Hopkins and King (2010) use content analysis to ascertain the tone of digital texts (blog posts). Their created *R* program codes the entire text with a tone of either –2 (extremely negative), –1 (negative), 0 (neutral), 1 (positive), or 2 (extremely positive). This will not work for presidential speeches because each individual speech may contain *content* that is totally unrelated to the *economy*, the population parameter of the data gathering. Moreover, one cannot create a data file of key vocabulary words addressing the economy that transcends time and provides comprehensibility.

5. Even Eshbaugh-Soha and Peake's (2011) analysis of presidential economic leadership of the media and public does not consider every term or issue that the presidents have mentioned that is associated with the economy. Suffice it to say, their analysis is quite extensive and yet, it is still not comprehensive.

6. *The American Presidency Project* is the largest online database of presidential documentation. John T. Woolley and Gerhard Peters, at the University of California, Santa Barbara, used a National Science Foundation Grant to digitize the public statements and documents of every president. It is a searchable and coded online database. *Policy Agendas Project*. (2014). "The data used here were originally collected by Frank R. Baumgartner and Bryan D. Jones, with the support of National Science Foundation grant numbers SBR 9320922 and 0111611, and were distributed through the Department of Government at the University of Texas at Austin. Neither NSF nor the original collectors of the data bear any responsibility for the analysis reported here."

7. See Riffe, Lacy, and Fico (2005) for published research that employs the same standards.

CHAPTER THREE

Presidential Rhetoric and the Federal Reserve

I thought I was the president, but when it comes to these bureaucrats, I can't do a damn thing.

—Harry S. Truman (Nathan, 1983)

The President and the Federal Reserve

Presidential administrations are highly concerned with what the Federal Reserve (Fed) does (Cohen and Hamman, 2003). This independent bureaucratic agency, created in 1913, is charged with being the central bank of the United States; it is supposed to maximize employment, moderate long-term interest rates, set monetary policy, and manage inflation by raising and/or lowering interest rates on monies loaned to banks, which substantially affects the overall economy (Auerbach, 1985; Dolan, Frendreis, and Tatalovich, 2008; Frumkin, 2004; Krause, 1994; Morris, 2000; Morris and Munger, 1998; Shull, 2005). Therefore, presidents have been trying to garner influence with the Fed since its inception (Worsham, 1997).

As many presidents do, Nixon often talked about the proper balance between inflation and unemployment and the Fed's role in bringing about what is necessary for a healthy economy, particularly the Federal Funds Rate (FFR), which when raised or lowered can stave off inflation or a recession. President Nixon went to great lengths to influence the decisions and monetary policy of the Fed during his chairmanship. In fact, Arthur F. Burns was nominated, in part, because it was thought that he would listen to Nixon and follow monetary policy directions from the administration. President Nixon, at the swearing in of Fed Chairman Burns, said "I do have the opportunity as president to convey my views to the chairman of the Federal Reserve." Moreover, the president indicated that he had "some very strong views on some of [the] economic matters . . ." and that he could "assure . . . that [he would] convey them privately and strongly to Dr. Burns." He continued by saying that he "hope[ed] that independently [Dr. Burns would] conclude that [President Nixon's] views are the ones that should be followed" (Woolley and Peters, 2014—"Richard Nixon, 1970").

President Nixon never tried to hide or mask his attempts to "influence" the independent agency in its decisions pertaining to the direction of monetary policy. Nixon is known to have said to Arthur Burns, "I know there's the myth of the autonomous Fed . . . and when you go up for confirmation some Senator may ask you about your friendship with the president. Appearances are going to be important" (Abrams, 2006). There are numerous recorded conversations that illustrate Nixon's attempts to influence the chairman and the agency. The following are quotes from Abrams (2006):

> October 23, 1969
> My relations with the Fed, will be different than they were with [previous Federal Reserve chairman] Bill Martin there. He was always six months too late doing anything. I'm counting on you, Arthur, to keep us out of a recession.
>
> October 10, 1971
> I don't want to go out of town [losing the presidential election] fast . . . this will be the last Conservative administration in Washington.
>
> December 24, 1971
> Do you feel, as far as Arthur [Federal Reserve chairman] and the money supply, we got that about as far as we can turn it right now, have we? I mean as far as my influence on him, that's what I'm really asking.
>
> February 14, 1972
> War is going to be declared if he [Chairman Arthur Burns] doesn't come around some.
>
> February 14, 1972
> I don't much, I really don't care what you [Arthur Burns] do in April, but between now and April . . . that can hurt us . . . in November.

Abrams (2006) indicates, however, from recorded conversations between President Nixon and George Shultz (Director of OMB), that the White

House received a firm commitment from Chairman Burns to expand monetary policy.

The speculation that Nixon was able to exert influence over the Fed and get them to acquiesce to an expansionary monetary policy and agenda seems to have a semblance of legitimacy. The accusations abounded during Arthur F. Burns tenure as Federal Reserve chairman, suggesting the Fed followed the directions and pressures from the president. According to William Safire, Nixon's speechwriter, the pressures extended to leaking negative newspaper stories about Burns's personal life so that he would toe the line (Abrams, 2006). Moreover, there were threats to change the number of members on the Fed's Federal Open Market Committee (FOMC). This would have given Nixon an opportunity to change the "majority," which would have given him more leverage to expand credit and the money supply (Abrams, 2006).

A few Nixon administration officials stated that the chairman had the FFR changed, as a result of the pressure, to facilitate in the advancement of President Nixon's agenda and reelection. Chairman Burns is recorded as saying, in multiple instances, "I wanted you [President Nixon] to know that we lowered the discount rate . . . got it down to 4.5 percent" (Abrams, 2006). Again, he tells the president that the FOMC was put "on notice that through this action that [he] want[s] more aggressive steps taken by [the] committee on next Tuesday"—indicating that he is following President Nixon's directions (Abrams, 2006). Abrams (2006) says, "the economic data supports the view that the Federal Reserve had already become decidedly more expansionary as Burns had promised."

After the 1972 election and later when President Nixon had resigned, the economy progressively soured, inflation reached over 12 percent, and a recession followed (Abrams, 2006; Bartlett, 2004). Many blamed Chairman Burns for the declining economy; he was an esteemed economist and had to be aware of the economic consequences of expanding the monetary policy. Abrams (2006) says,

> Without invoking political pressure, the surge of expansionary monetary policy leading up to the 1972 election seems hard to explain. After all, Arthur Burns knew better than to run a heavily expansive monetary policy after the recession had ended in November 1970 and in an already-inflationary environment.

Nevertheless, a researcher can never fully ascertain if Chairman Burns succumbed to the pressure from President Nixon, aside from him stating clearly that he did. Chairman Burns was highly intelligent and understood the economy; he simply could have done what he thought was the right thing to do in terms of economic policy. Despite his intelligence and economic skills, his actions could have been incorrect. Moreover, the phone conversations could easily be explained by saying that Chairman Burns was telling the president what he wanted to hear while on the phone and then pursuing what he thought was the best course of action at the Fed. There are other conversations wherein President Nixon emphatically expresses his distrust of Burns and others wherein Burns expresses his ideals for economic policy to Nixon. As a matter of fact, however, the FFR did change during the time in question.

Arthur Burns joined the Federal Reserve on February 1, 1971, during a time when the FFR was steadily decreasing, beginning the process of expanding the amount of money available and keeping inflation down. Expanding the amount of money was directly in line with what Nixon wanted, as he thought the Fed's decision to contract the economy precluded his presidential victory in 1960 (Abrams, 2006). Nixon said prior to the election in 1972,

> Arthur Burns, in terms of monetary policy and in terms of fiscal policy, has followed a course that I think is the most responsible and statesmanlike of any chairman of the Federal Reserve in my memory. In other words, you have seen an expansionary monetary policy, and that is one of the reasons we have had an expansionary economy in the first six months of this year. (Woolley and Peters, 2014—"Richard Nixon, 1971")

In that same speech, President Nixon may have shown his hand in a very revealing manner when he said, "So we find that Burns agrees—that I agree with Burns, let's put it that way. I agree with Burns very strongly on his monetary policy, on his fiscal policy" (Woolley and Peters, 2014—"Richard Nixon, 1971").

History is riddled with instances, anecdotal however, wherein the decisions of the Fed have mirrored the wishes of the sitting president. Given the Fed's noted independence from political control, whether the president influenced the Fed is noteworthy, given our understanding and commitment to separated institutions sharing power. Nixon's comments and Chairman Burns's decisions warrant further and more comprehensive inquiry into whether or not Arthur Burns used his position as chairman of the Fed to get the FOMC to change the FFR and the direction of monetary policy, at the expense of the economic health of the United States, to aid in Nixon's reelection.

The following chapter offers a quantitative explanation regarding presidential influence with one of the most significant economic actors. How can the president assert influence over one incredibly important aspect of the economy if he cannot even get the economic actor to listen to him? The findings serve to highlight the glaring flaw in the prevailing argument that presidential rhetoric matters in the sense that it can persuade or influence—as the most important economic actors are not even paying attention to what the president is saying. The findings provide a contribution to the contentious discussion in the literature on presidential relations with the Federal Reserve regarding the president's capacity to influence monetary policy (Beck, 1982; Havrilesky, 1995; Krause, 1994; Maisel, 1973; Morris, 2000; Nathan, 1983; Weintraub, 1978; Wood and Waterman, 1994).

Nevertheless, I consider the literature regarding the limitations presidential appointments to the Federal Reserve Board have and address how presidential rhetoric factors into the Fed's decision-making regarding monetary policy. From ascertaining the overall ineffectiveness of presidential rhetoric and signals to the Fed, I posit a theory and empirical model that suggests the Federal Reserve is more responsive to Congress and current economic conditions when making monetary policy decisions.

Garnering Influence with the Federal Reserve

In order to gain influence over the economy, particularly monetary policy, presidents often try to put pressure on the Fed, using every mechanism their office and institution afford to them (Howell, 2003; Havrilesky, 1995). Presidents typically try to shape the Fed with appointments to the seven-member board of governors. Moreover, presidents often use cues and signals to the Fed to indicate what direction they want them to take monetary policy. Typically, the cues consist of changes in fiscal policy and calls for the Fed to address inflation or unemployment, areas that substantively impact the economy.

Historically, there is a desire for presidents to influence the Fed; however, there is considerable disagreement about the extent to which the influence is successful or effective (Auerbach, 1985; Beck, 1982; Havrilesky, 1995; Krause, 1994; Maisel, 1973; Morris, 2000; Nathan, 1983; Weintraub, 1978; Wood and Waterman, 1994). According to many scholars, presidents have struggled to garner influence with the Fed, partly because it is an independent agency (Chappell, Havrilesky, and McGregor, 1993; Cohen and Hamman, 2005; Havrilesky, 1995; Morris, 2000; Munger and Roberts, 1990; Wood and Waterman, 1994). For instance, the discretion by the Fed, where their localities lie, and to whom they are accountable are all factors that keep scholars continually trying to model this relationship and ascertain insight into who is able to pressure the Fed and their monetary policy decision-making (Brehm and Gates, 1997).

Appointments

Presidents attempt to use appointments to shape the monetary policy decisions at the Fed (Beck, 1982; Dolan, Frendreis, and Tatalovich, 2008; Krause, 1994). There is a vast literature claiming presidents are effective at doing this (Chappell, Havrilesky, and McGregor, 1993; Golden, 2000; Havrilesky, 1995; Havrilesky and Gildea, 1992; Nathan, 1983; Waterman, 1989; Wood and Waterman, 1994). There are still substantive gaps, however, in the arguments, which have not done a satisfactory job of explaining the presidential influence with the Fed empirically and comprehensively (Munger and Roberts, 1990). There seems to be an assumption that presidents are able to influence monetary policy with their appointments (Auerbach, 1985; Hibbs, 1987; Maisel, 1973; Weintraub, 1978).

The decisions that the Fed makes can sabotage or undermine the policy goals of the presidents (Brehm and Gates, 1997). In addition, the structure of the relationship allows the Fed to achieve agency-oriented goals, which are purely self-interested (Downs, 1967). This means that the requests that come from the president are not precisely what will be pursued and implemented at the Fed. Moreover, even though it features a seven-member board of governors, appointed by the president, there is no guarantee that the appointees will remain loyal to the policies of the president (Edwards and Wayne, 1985). Many appointees in bureaucratic agencies "go native" once they are immersed in the agency culture and begin advocating for the plans of the agency rather than those of the president who appointed them (DiClerico, 2000).

While, such a statement is somewhat true, one has to consider the subtleties of the appointment process to obtain a more accurate picture of the degree to which appointments empower presidents to shape monetary policy (Keech and Morris, 1997). Upon further inquiry, the realities of presidential influence at the Fed are significantly less potent than commonly assumed (Keech and Morris, 1997).

Chappell, Havrilesky, and McGregor (1993), as discussed in Keech and Morris (1997), argue that Democratic presidents, more than Republican presidents, typically appoint those members who prefer lower interest rates. This fact, they claim, enables presidents to "pack" the Fed with like-minded persons who will then change Fed monetary policy. The reality, however, is that presidents have not enjoyed the opportunity to appoint majorities to the Fed board of governors very often (Keech and Morris, 1997). As illustrated by table 3.1, presidents spend most of their time in office, in fact, before they are able to make enough appointments to have a majority at the Fed.

To further complicate the "packing" argument, presidents must contend with the "Earl Warren Effect" when making appointments to the Fed—namely appointees completely follow a different policy path than the one desired by the appointing president (Morris, 2000, p. 73). Havrilesky and

Table 3.1. Presidential Appointments to the Board of Governors.

	Membership of the Federal Reserve System (1953–2012)	
D. D. Eisenhower 1953–1961	Wm. McC. Martin, Jr. 1956–1970 C. Canby Balderston 1954–1966 Chas. N. Shepardson 1955–1967	A. L. Mills, Jr. 1958–1965 Paul E. Miller 1954–1954 G. H. King, Jr. 1959–1963
J. F. Kennedy 1961–1963	George W. Mitchell 1961–1976	
L. B. Johnson 1963–1969	J. Dewey Daane 1963–1974 Andrew F. Brimmer 1966–1974	Sherman J. Maisel 1965–1972 William W. Sherrill 1967–1971
R. M. Nixon 1969–1974	Arthur Burns 1970–1978 Jeffrey M. Bucher 1972–1976 Henry C. Wallich 1974–1986	John E. Sheehan 1972–1975 Robert C. Holland 1973–1976
G. R. Ford 1974–1977	Philip E. Coldwell 1974–1980 J. Charles Partee 1976–1986 David M. Lilly 1976–1978	Philip C. Jackson, Jr. 1975–1978 Stephen S. Gardner 1976–1978
J. E. Carter 1977–1981	G. William Miller 1978–1979 Emmett J. Rice 1979–1986 Paul A. Volcker 1979–1987	Nancy H. Teeters 1978–1984 Frederick H. Schultz 1979–1982 Lyle E. Gramley 1980–1985
R. W. Reagan 1981–1989	Preston Martin 1982–1986 Wayne D. Angell 1986–1994 H. Robert Heller 1986–1989 Alan Greenspan 1987–2006	Martha R. Seger 1984–1991 Manuel H. Johnson 1986–1990 Edward W. Kelley, Jr. 1987–2001 John P. LaWare 1988–1995
G. H. W. Bush 1989–1993	David W. Mullins, Jr. 1990–1994 Susan M. Phillips 1991–1998	Lawrence B. Lindsey 1991–1997
W. J. Clinton 1993–2001	Alan Greenspan 1987–2006 Janet L. Yellen 1994–1997 Alice M. Rivlin 1996–1999 Edward M. Gramlich 1997–2005	Alan S. Blinder 1994–1996 Laurence H. Meyer 1996–2002 Roger W. Ferguson, Jr. 1997–2006
G. W. Bush 2001–2009	Roger W. Ferguson, Jr. 1997–2006 Mark W. Olson 2001–2006 Donald L. Kohn 2002–2010 Randall S. Kroszner 2006–2009 Elizabeth A. Duke 2008–2013	Susan S. Bies 2001–2007 Ben S. Bernanke 2002–2006 Kevin M. Warsh 2006–2011 Frederic S. Mishkin 2006–2008
B. H. Obama 2009–	Daniel K. Tarullo 2009– Janet L. Yellen 2010– Jeremy C. Stein 2012–	Sarah Bloom Raskin 2010– Jerome H. Powell 2012–

Adapted from Federal Reserve Official Website, 2014.

Gildea (1992) found that from 1951–1987 the presidential appointments to the Fed's FOMC did not always vote for the policy preferences of those presidents who appointed them.

Moreover, appointments to the Fed are similar to appointments to the Supreme Court; there has to be agreement with the political, business, and economic communities in order to secure a position on the Fed Board (Beck, 1982). Divided government and election proximity keep partisan appointees from confirmation by the Senate (Waller, 1992). In fact, many of the appointments are persons who have risen through the ranks at the Fed; they are not politically partisan appointments from campaign staff, but rather "experts" who have already been "institutionalized" at the Fed.

Just as important, presidential appointments do not provide any significant level of influence over the Fed's FOMC's decision-making when compared to the influence that takes place from within the Fed, particularly with regard to consensus within the FOMC and the Fed chair (Krause, 1994). Presidential appointments of the chair of the Fed are not correlated with significant changes in Fed monetary policy (Beck, 1987; Chang, 2001; Krause, 1994; Maisel, 1973; Nordhaus, 1975; Rose, 1991; Tufte, 1978). Moreover, there is also no substantive evidence that appointments to the Fed's FOMC had any influence on policy either (Chang, 2001).

Where there is change in the predicted median influence, the data do not tell us if the influence is coming from the president or the Senate, who may be, and often are, at odds with one another (Chang, 2001). In the instances where there were substantial changes to the Fed's monetary policy, it is more likely that the changes were a result of external pressures from Congress or the changing/shifting world economy rather than a result of presidential appointments, policy preferences, or rhetorical cues from the president (Beck, 1982; Saeki and Shull, 2003).

Based upon the extant empirical literature, there is no theoretical justification to include appointments into the following statistical model. The extant research does a thorough job refuting the notion that presidents can influence monetary policy with appointments to the Fed. Nevertheless, I included this section to highlight the fact that even a concrete power that the president has with the Fed does not grant him influence over the agency or their decision-making. If the appointment power does not afford the president's influence, the likelihood that rhetoric does is even less probable.

Granted, one could argue that the Fed might pay attention to what the president says and act accordingly with regard to the FFR when there is a vacancy in the hopes that the president will appoint someone of which the Fed approves. However, I discuss this and the literature later. The president is going to appoint someone that the Senate will confirm. Therefore, it is not likely that the Fed would go against what Congress wants in an attempt to get some shortsighted gain, because, in fact, the president is not really going to go against what the Senate wants due to the fact that he knows the person would not likely obtain confirmation anyway.

Rhetorical Cues and Signals

The president of the Federal Reserve Bank of Chicago, along with many of his colleagues, believes that the stimulation needed to make the economy better occurs by changing the way elite economic policymakers talk about the best direction for the economy (Campbell, Evans, Fisher, and Justiniano, 2012). Given their position and the size of the president's constituencies, it seems to assert that presidents would be able to influence this particular economic actor directly with cues and signals.

More importantly, there are instances where Fed chairmen have stated that presidential requests and cues have changed the behavior of the Fed, particularly during the Johnson administration (see table 3.2). There are also a few claims in the literature stating that the Fed has manipulated the FFR during elections to either help or hurt the incumbent president, as discussed earlier (Beck, 1987; Maisel, 1973; Nordhaus, 1975; Tufte, 1978). These claims were prevalent during the election of 1972. Many of those supposedly

Table 3.2. Presidential Administrations and the Chairpersons of the Fed.

	Federal Reserve System (1953–2012)	
William McChesney Martin, Jr.	Dwight D. Eisenhower	John F. Kennedy
1951–1970	Lyndon B. Johnson	Richard M. Nixon
Arthur F. Burns	Gerald R. Ford	James "Jimmy" E. Carter
1970–1978		
G. William Miller	James "Jimmy" E. Carter	
1978–1979		
Paul A. Volcker	Ronald W. Reagan	
1979–1987		
Alan Greenspan	George H. W. Bush	William J. Clinton
1987–2006	George W. Bush	
Ben Bernanke	George W. Bush	Barack H. Obama
2006–2014		
Janet Yellen	Barack H. Obama	
2014–		

Adapted from Federal Reserve Official Website, 2014.

involved either denied the accusations or recanted later what had been said (Beck, 1982).

When controlling for the president and the Fed chairman, however, there is a statistical effect for changes in monetary policy (Havrilesky, 1995). The response of monetary policy to signals does not continue for all presidents and chairmen; it only exists for certain periods. For instance, the FFR changed when Arthur Burns was the chairman under presidents Nixon and Ford, but not when it was William Martin. The same chairman with the Carter administration shows no influence. When President Carter switched to Chairman Volcker, the monetary policy did react to the signals. This continued through the first Reagan administration, but not the second. When Chairman Greenspan took over, monetary policy responded to the signals from President Reagan. This trend did not continue with President George H. W. Bush and Chairman Greenspan. Interestingly, however, monetary policy did respond to President Clinton's signals when Chairman Greenspan was there. Monetary policy briefly followed the direction of President George W. Bush with Chairman Greenspan. Finally, there is no question that monetary policy followed the direction President Obama desired while Chairman Bernanke is at the helm, and seems to be currently following Chairwoman Yellen.

These anecdotal examples, however, do not withstand statistical scrutiny, such evidence has not been proven to be a comprehensive and systematic statistical reality, but rather appears to be "episodic" with most such claims unsubstantiated by empirical findings (Beck, 1982; Havrilesky, 1995, p. 37).

However, there are a number of reasons why the president will use signals as a mechanism of successful economic leadership to the Fed (Eshbaugh-Soha, 2006; Wood, 2007). Informing the Fed of his policy preferences is the best, most effective way for the president to overcome the coalition building challenges as well as the vitriolic political process (DiClerico, 2000). The president wants to signal to the "policy elites" for what he is willing to fight, such as a contractionary or expansionary monetary policy and provide reassurances of how much commitment he has to his economic/monetary policy (Eshbaugh-Soha, 2006; p. 7). This opportunity enables the president to signal the economic groups and policymakers about how their actions will be recompensed (Eshbaugh-Soha, 2005).

The prevailing theories and research states that the president's ability to employ rhetoric to shape the behavior of economic actors should be substantiated by the fact that the president is the foremost person with economic information, which makes him the most visible figure in economic discussions (Eshbaugh-Soha, 2005; Wood, 2007). The fact that the president has the largest staff of economic actors (National Economic Council, Council of Economic Advisors (CEA), Office of Management and Budget, Department of Treasury, Department of Commerce, Department of Labor, Bureau of Economic Analysis) providing him with information and advice makes him appear to be the preeminent economic policymaker. The expectation is that the president, because of his access to comprehensive information, leads the economy, particularly through downturns and prosperity, with rhetoric, signals, and cues (Wood, 2004). Should this unparalleled role give him a direct influence over the economy? In other words, should the Fed be responsive to his rhetoric, looking to him for direction, information, and leadership?

Presidents use rhetoric to assert their power and position. Thus, does it make it an influential mechanism of presidential power? Sending positive and negative signals to the Fed is the president's way of conveying his policy preferences (Eshbaugh-Soha, 2006; Eshbaugh-Soha and Peake, 2005). The president hopes the economic speeches function as his mechanism of power, an instrument of the modern presidency that conveys what he wants. He hopes the signals put pressure on the Fed to act (Eshbaugh-Soha, 2006). Successfully influencing the Fed, however, is profoundly complicated because they are independent so presidents have to rely on their ability to persuade them to make decisions about complex and controversial policies: employment, prices, long-term interest rates, raising interest rates or lowering interest rates (Beck, 1982; Dolan, Frendreis, and Tatalovich, 2008; Havrilesky, 1995; Krause, 1994; Maisel, 1973; Morris, 2000; Weintraub, 1978; Wood and Waterman, 1994).

The Fed's Response to Cues and Signals

The signals are, typically, verbal words or cues that presidents speak to the policy elites. These signals can offer support for specific programs or they can be expressions of their opposition to what the policy elites are actually doing. Moreover, the signals can be specific such as requests for changes or actions to an existing policy. As long as the president is informing the elites of his preferences, what he is doing is a signal (Eshbaugh-Soha, 2006).

The cues and signals presidents use can be found in the literature on what the Fed does economically, the attention it pays to unemployment, inflation, and the interest rates (Dolan, Frendreis, and Tatalovich, 2008; Eshbaugh-Soha, 2006). The most pertinent economic indicators, or policy tools as the Fed calls them, help to make up the U.S. monetary policy, which can make or break a president's legacy, reelection, or image to the "Washingtonians" (Havrilesky, 1995; Neustadt, 1991). Shaping monetary policy is crucial for presidential success (Morris, 2000). The cues and signals to the Fed ensure that the president is, in fact, trying to influence the behavior of this particular economic actor.

Should the Fed be receptive of the president's signals because of cue taking; their rhetoric is a form of leadership signaling (Whitford and Yates, 2009)? Do the signals and cues to the Fed engender "cognitive shortcuts" in relation to information that is pertinent to the agency (Eshbaugh-Soha, 2006, p. 38)? Elite policymakers have limited information about the political ramifications of most policy decisions. By listening to the president, are the policy elites able to make effective decisions about policy because the president fills in that information that is lacking, due to his vast network?

The prevailing theories suggests that presidential signals, consistent speeches about the state of the economy, and the president's policy preferences for the Fed inform the agency of the president's positions and economic goals (Eshbaugh-Soha, 2005). Using signals that address issues of concern to the Fed, the president should be able to influence their decision-making. The tone of the speeches filters through to the economic actors and should be reflected in their economic behavior, which creates a consistent message that can "establish a climate for economic perceptions" (Wood, 2007, p. 14). This climate is something that the president can then manipulate or shape, according to Wood (2007).

In order to measure whether the Fed is responsive to the signals of the president, Havrilesky (1995) created a "SAFER index," coding every mention in the *Wall Street Journal* that addressed monetary policy (expansionary or contractionary) and some action mentioned by other members of the president's administration such as the Secretary of Treasury and the CEA (p. 118). He found no statistically significant impact in the period 1964–1994, when controlling for the White House staff and the CEA. The study only looked at one, fairly conservative, economic newspaper, rather than a comprehensive timespan of presidential comments (Gentzkow and Shapiro, 2006; Woods and Arthur, 2014). Moreover, it is fair to assume that the *Wall Street Journal* is going to mention only those comments they find pertinent to the overall goals of their newspaper (Eshbaugh-Soha and Peake, 2008).

Moreover, the Clinton administration's signals to the bond market did not make a significant difference; there was no effect on the thirty-year Treasury Bills despite the rhetoric (Eshbaugh-Soha, 2005). President George H. W. Bush's signals to the market about the money supply in his State of the Union Addresses were not effective (Eshbaugh-Soha, 2005). In fact, his signals returned the opposite outcomes. He does, however, find that there is an effect when he controls for the president and the Fed chairman (Havrilesky, 1995). The response of monetary policy to signals does not continue for all presidents and chairmen; it only exists for certain periods.

Such data and results suggest that the president has a limited influence over economic and monetary policy (Eshbaugh-Soha, 2005). Moreover, studies show that in the pre-golden (1953–1962), golden (1963–1985), and the post-golden (1986–2002) age television eras, presidential rhetoric had no significant effect on how the public viewed economic policy (Young and Perkins, 2005). The research suggests that the presidents, through their rhetorical actions, are limited in their ability to influence economic effects or economic indicators directly.

Scholarship really has no comprehensive evidence detailing the extent to which presidents send signals to the Fed about economic policy, despite a complex and growing literature on presidential signals to various actors, and subsequently, no comprehensive evidence suggesting the extent to which the Fed responds to the presidential rhetoric (Whitford and Yates, 2009; Wood, 2007). Therefore, assessing the Fed's responsiveness to the signals in a comprehensive analysis provides an important look into the effectiveness of presidential rhetoric to shape economic and monetary policy at the Fed. If positivity and/or negativity can predict changes in the FFR, then one can confidently state that the presidents have the ability to shape the economic behavior of the Fed. The following model and hypotheses offer insight into the limitations the aforementioned theory has regarding the president's ability to influence the Fed with signals and rhetoric.

Hypotheses for Predicting Changes in the Federal Funds Rate

The data gathered for this particular analysis show that presidents try to signal the Fed, however, based upon the political realities of their relationship with the Fed and the limitations such a relationship imposes on the president, they struggle to do so effectively. The statistical model will offer results that suggest the aggregated, positive economic rhetoric from the president is unable to shape the behavior of the Fed, changes in the FFR (Dolan, Frendreis, and Tatalovich, 2008). The expectation is that presidential rhetoric is not able to predict the probability that the Fed will change the FFR.

> $H1_O$: The president's positive economic rhetoric will predict the probability that the Fed will *change* the FFR.

$H1_A$: The Fed will respond to the president's positive economic rhetoric either by leaving the FFR where it is or the Fed will lower the FFR.

$H2_O$: The president's negative economic rhetoric will predict the probability that the Fed will *lower* the FFR.

$H2_A$: The Fed will respond to the president's negative economic rhetoric either by leaving the FFR where it is or the Fed will raise the FFR.

Congressional Pressures on the Federal Reserve

Some have argued that the Fed is more likely to make decisions about monetary policy based upon external pressures from Congress rather than cues or signals from the president (Saeki and Shull, 2003). Congress often requires that members of the board of governors provide testimony before hearings and particular committees about the economy and future economic conditions (Saeki and Shull, 2003). More specifically, the preferences of the Senate play a significant role in the Fed's decision to adopt an expansionary or a restrictive monetary policy (Morris, 2000). The senators are going to have specific preferences based upon the preferences of their constituents and their party ideology (Saeki and Shull, 2003).

The Fed is less likely to choose a direction for monetary policy that would encounter opposition in Congress, which has asserted its authority and made transparency a major requirement due to the secrecy with which the Fed conducted its monetary policy decision-making in the past (Havrilesky, 1995; Munger and Roberts, 1990). The Fed is now required to present, to Congress, its thoughts regarding the FFR and the direction it believes the economy is headed. The Fed acquiesced to these demands rather than fighting; it feared how aggressively Congress would assert its authority and how much autonomy they could potentially lose (Havrilesky, 1995).

The Fed responds to the policy preferences of Congress; they have the most influence in the Fed's role with monetary policy (Havrilesky, 1995; Munger and Roberts, 1990). More specifically, the Fed is going to pay significant attention to the chairperson of the Senate Banking Committee (SBC) when considering whether they will expand or contract monetary policy, given the power of this chairperson: autonomy, agenda-setting, and ability to call hearings, as well as the chairperson's ability to withstand pressure to compromise on their ideological predilections, unlike the president who has a national constituency (Saeki and Shull, 2003). The Fed is more likely to make its decision about the economy based upon the preferences of the SBC chairperson rather than the president (Saeki and Shull, 2003).

The prevailing thought, entrenched in the literature, is that Republicans advocate for contractionary monetary policy (higher interest rates) and that Democrats seek after expansionary monetary policy (lower interest rates), as these approaches best favor their respective constituencies (Havrilesky, 1995; Hibbs, 1987; Keech and Morris, 1997). In other words, the ideology of the political parties plays a major role in the monetary policy the Fed pursues (Hibbs, 1987). Particularly, the Senators are going to have specific preferences based upon their constituents and the necessities of their reelection attempt (Saeki and Shull, 2003). This is overwhelmingly seen in the fact that Democratic presidents typically appoint those members who prefer lower interest rates more than Republican appointees (Chappell, Havrilesky, and McGregor, 1993). This must be factored into the discussion given that the Senate must confirm each of the appointees to the Fed's board of governors.

Congressional intervention into monetary policy mitigates the influence the president has over the Fed (Havrilesky, 1995). Congress exercises a significant influence over the FFR when it communicates its policy preferences in the biannual Congressional Oversight Hearings on monetary policy (Havrilesky, 1995). Therefore, this analysis seeks to determine if the Fed makes changes to the FFR, as a result of the political party of the chairperson of the SBC or the number of hearings the Congress has regarding the economy, particularly since the literature indicates that the Congress asserts institutional pressures on the Fed regarding policy.

> $H3_O$: The political party of the chairperson of the SBC will predict the type of economic policy the Fed will pursue in its decisions to *change* the FFR.
>
> $H3_A$: The Fed will respond to the political party of the chairperson of the SBC by leaving the FFR where it is or pursuing a contractionary or expansionary monetary policy with disregard to party ideology.
>
> $H4_O$: The number of congressional hearings regarding the economy will predict the probability that the Fed will alter its economic behavior and *change* the FFR.
>
> $H4_A$: The Fed will respond to the number of congressional hearings regarding the economy either by leaving the FFR where it is or pursuing a contractionary or expansionary monetary policy with disregard to congressional attention to the economy.

The Federal Reserve's Attention to Economic Conditions

Presidents have not addressed the economy in a major way in five of the last eleven recessions. In fact, presidents speak more about noneconomic-related issues during a recession than economic issues (Hoffman and Howard, 2010). They tend to offer fewer speeches during times of recession, inflation, and low employment (Ragsdale, 1987). There is a reason for this: constructing too dramatic a picture of the economy can have seriously negative effects for the president. Moreover, presenting the economy as better than it actually is or ignoring the realities makes the president seem out of touch or incompetent, both of which can affect his interaction with important political actors or the electorate (Hoffman and Howard, 2010). They rarely, if ever, make major economic speeches to inform the public how well the economy is doing.

The state of the economy accounts for public perceptions of the effectiveness of political actors (Wood, 2007). According to Dolan, Frendreis, and Tatalovich (2008), the public expects the government to keep the economy feasible. Despite particular events of national importance, the economy, specifically unemployment and inflation, top Gallup's "Most Important Problem" every year since 1936. The economy is important to the public, and they have substantively linked their perceptions of its condition to their own personal political behavior. Downturns in the economy affect the agenda, reelections, and public perceptions of the president. Moreover, the president's party typically loses congressional seats when the economy is not satisfactory (Dolan, Frendreis, and Tatalovich, 2008).

As stated in the Federal Reserve Act of 1913, the Fed is supposed to maximize employment, stable prices, and moderate long-term interest rates (Dolan, Frendreis, and Tatalovich, 2008). This legislative mandate allows the Fed to substantively affect inflation. Economic conditions must be considered a pertinent motivator for the Fed's decisions to change the FFR (Saeki and Shull, 2003). The Fed has a legislative responsibility to pursue low unemployment and low inflation, which makes it more likely to consider these rates when deciding whether to raise or lower the FFR (Beck, 1982). These indicators can better explain the monetary policy changes rather than the president's cues, especially when you consider the Fed's institutional pride and legacy (Beck, 1982).

> $H5_O$: The Fed will respond to the changes in GDP (threats of recession) by modifying the FFR to combat inflation and unemployment.

> $H5_A$: The Fed will use the FFR to pursue a contractionary or expansionary monetary policy with disregard to the changes in GDP.

> $H6_O$: The Fed will respond to the changes in the inflation rate by modifying the FFR to combat inflation and unemployment.

$H6_A$: The Fed will use the FFR to pursue a contractionary or expansionary monetary policy with disregard to the changes in the inflation rate.

$H7_O$: The Fed will respond to the changes in the unemployment rate by modifying the FFR to combat inflation and unemployment.

$H7_A$: The Fed will use the FFR to pursue a contractionary or expansionary monetary policy with disregard to the changes in the unemployment rate.

Empirical Model

As per the hypotheses above, three models (M1 = the tone of presidential rhetoric, M2 = congressional attention to the economy, and M3 = economic indicators) were constructed to ascertain the conditions that can create changes in the FFR.[1] Using content analysis, the rhetorical cues and signals the presidents sent to the Fed were coded according to a detailed protocol and codebook, as discussed in chapter 1. The *Policy Agendas Project* data on congressional hearings were manipulated to match this model. And, the economic data were gathered from the Bureau of Labor Statistics (BLS). Each model allowed me to estimate the effects of these independent variables on the FFR. The time series analysis was for every president from Dwight D. Eisenhower (1954) through Barack H. Obama (2012), as illustrated by figure 3.1. The unit of analysis was *monthly* for each model. For the regression analysis involving presidential rhetoric, I estimated two lags; each is a month in duration. I chose to use a monthly lag because the dependent variable is estimated monthly. Moreover, I chose to use only two of these lags because the literature justifies such an action. There are time limits on the effectiveness and potency of presidential rhetoric (Edwards, 2003; 2009; Whitford and Yates, 2009). The policy window of any salient issue the president is discussing has limits with regard to the attention span of political actors and the public (Eshbaugh-Soha, 2006; Kingdon, 1995).

Statistical Method

As with many time series analyses, the Durbin-Watson statistical test in the Ordinary Least Squares (OLS) Regression Analysis presented first-order autocorrelation (AR1) in each model (d = 0.15 for M1, d = 0.22 for M2, and d = 0.11 for M3) (Comiskey and Marsh, 2012; Yates and Whitford, 2005). Based upon the diagnostics, using a Prais-Winston (1954) regression analysis with the Cochrane–Orcutt estimation allowed me to more appropriately estimate the changes in the FFR (Gerring, Thacker, and Moreno, 2005; Gronke and Miller, 2012; Lowry and Shipan, 2002; Whitford and Ochs, 2006; Yates

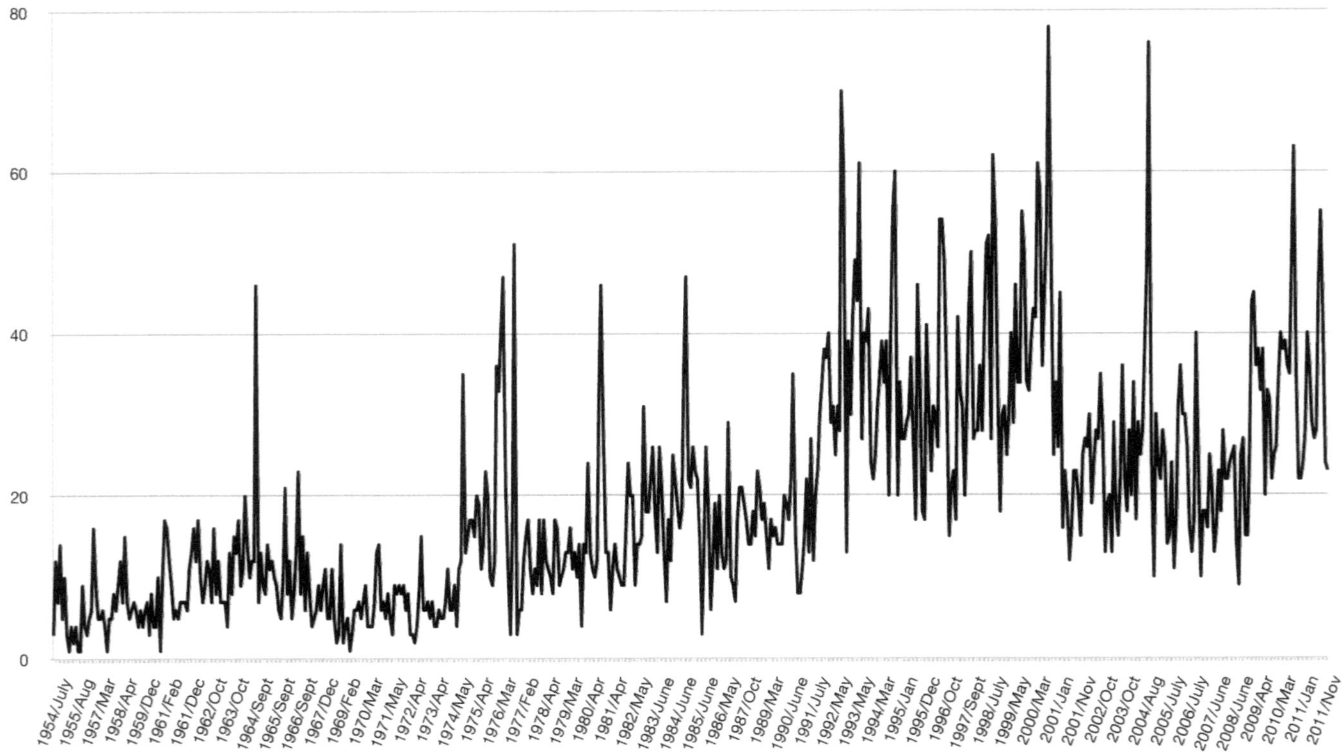

Figure 3.1. Monthly Totals of Presidential Speeches July 1954–January 2012.
Adapted from *The American Presidency Project*, 2014.

and Whitford, 2005). Moreover, the variance inflation factor (VIF) results indicated that there was no problem with multicollinearity in either of the models and I estimated the regressions with semirobust standard errors after respecifying the model to mitigate any residual heterskedasticity. The model, overall, is in line with the hypotheses[2]; the predictor variables in this analysis do not significantly affect whether the Fed changes its FFR as a result of the positivity and/or negativity in the president's economic rhetoric. However, as theorized, the results suggest that the FFR does respond to congressional behavior and economic indicators.

Independent Variables

Presidential Economic Rhetoric (M1)

Identifying the presidential rhetoric aimed at the Fed was, again, accomplished by using the *Public Papers of the President* in *The American Presidency Project*, from July 1954 through January 19, 2012. This provided the researcher with 1,530 presidential speeches. The population is measured over sixty-five years (1946–2012). The presidential cues and signals to the Federal Reserve were coded as the ratio of positive speeches to negative and neutral speeches (positive ratio [positive speeches]/[positive speeches + negative speeches + neutral speeches] and the ratio of negative speeches to positive and neutral speeches [negative ratio] [negative speeches]/[negative speeches + positive speeches + neutral speeches]). I created two, one-month lags for each of these variables.

Coding the speeches as "positive" must be differentiated from the notion of "optimism," which is perpetually present in presidential economic rhetoric; they are the economy's unremitting cheerleader. As illustrated by table 3.3, many of the positive mentions are presidential claims of moving the economy toward positive economic growth, such as creating jobs, mitigating the effects of inflation, lessening the burden to tax payers, or economic expansion. As shown by figures 3.4 and 3.5 later in the analysis, presidents are generally more positive about the economy and do not often discuss the "negative" economy.

For the first model (M1), I included more independent variables to help control for the effects of each of the other independent variables that influence the dependent variable (FFR). I included the actual number of total speeches given per month (1 to 78) in order to account for the amount of attention the president is paying to the economy. To better account for the attention, I broke the number of speeches down by tone and included the

Table 3.3. Example Sentences Measuring the Tone of Presidential Rhetoric.

	Speeches from The American Presidency Project
D. D. Eisenhower 1/18/1960	This budget attests to the strength of America's economy. At the same time, the budget is a test of our resolve, as a nation, to allocate our resources prudently, to maintain the Nation's security, and to extend economic growth into the future without inflation.
J. F. Kennedy 1/24/1963	The chief problem confronting our economy in 1963 is its unrealized potential—slow growth, underinvestment . . . and persistent unemployment.
L. B. Johnson 1/26/1967	Interest rates in 1966 were as high as at any time in forty years. They were pushed there by an insatiable demand for credit, straining against a deliberately restricted supply. Monetary policy in 1966—like tax policy—was properly aimed at slowing down an economy expanding too fast.
R. M. Nixon 8/15/1971	The tax reductions I am recommending, together with this broad upturn of the economy which has taken place in the first half of this year, will move us strongly forward toward a goal this nation has not reached since 1956, fifteen years ago: prosperity with full employment in peacetime.
G. R. Ford 12/3/1974	Admittedly, the American economy is in a recession at the present time. Inflation pressures are many. Fear of unemployment is increasing among our people.
J. E. Carter 1/21/1980	Inflation continues to be our most serious economic problem. Restraining inflation remains my highest domestic priority. Inflation at the current, unacceptably high levels is the direct result of economic problems that have been building, virtually without letup, for over a decade. There are no easy answers, or quick solutions to inflation. It cannot be eliminated overnight; its roots in our economy are too deep, its causes are too pervasive and complex.
R. W. Reagan 1/11/1989	Our plans for the economy would cause inflation to soar and bring about economic collapse.
G. H. W. Bush 2/12/1991	These shocks hit an economy that was already growing slowly for several reasons, including worldwide increases in interest rates, tightened credit conditions, and the lingering effects of a successful attempt begun in 1988 by the Federal Reserve to prevent an acceleration of inflation . . . I know that in some regions of our country, people are in genuine economic distress.
W. J. Clinton 6/6/1997	Today we received one more piece of solid evidence that this invest-and-grow strategy is working. We learned that our economy added 138,000 new jobs and that unemployment dropped to 4.8 percent, the lowest in twenty-four years.
G. W. Bush 5/22/2004	With the right policies, we will maintain the strong forward momentum of the American economy, which is creating thousands of new jobs for American workers.
B. H. Obama 2/24/2011	The economy is now growing. In many sectors we're seeing recovery. But the biggest challenge that we're seeing right now is the fact that unemployment is still way too high all across the country.

Adapted from *The American Presidency Project*, 2014.

number of negative speeches given per month (0 to 6) and the number of positive speeches given per month (0 to 9). Using the number of monthly presidential calls for legislation that deal with the economy (0 to 6) will further measure the presidential attempts to shape the economy. In addition to presidential attempts at shaping the economy, the presidents' party affiliations (Democrat [1 = yes or 0 = no]; Republican [1 = yes or 0 = no]) and their average approval ratings (expressed as a monthly percentage = 0 to 100 percent) complement the model and ensure that it is specified correctly.

Congressional Attention (M2)

The data at the *Policy Agendas Project* was used to assess congressional behavior in the second model (M2). These data provide the number of total congressional hearings on the economy and the number of SBC hearings from the 79th Congress to the 110th Congress. From this data, I was able to construct six independent variables that are pertinent to the analysis. As evidenced by figure 3.2, I aggregated, monthly, the total days of hearings on the economy to measure congressional attention to economic issues that are important to the Fed (0 to 57). Moreover, I was able to ascertain the number of hearings the SBC had regarding economic issues relating to the Fed's responsibilities (0 to 15). I excluded those hearings on the economy that had to do with appropriations and reauthorizations; including such elements will confuse the data and the results (Edwards and Wood, 1999).

In addition to measuring congressional attention to the economy, considering the importance of party is necessary to measure the differences of influence within the committees, particularly because majority parties have more resources at their disposal to arrange committees and shape the agenda, as illustrated by figure 3.2 (Aldrich and Rohde, 2000). Moreover, what matters are the preferences of individual members of Congress, particularly the median member; bills cannot garner institutional support until they pass the majority in the House and the filibuster threat in the Senate (Brady and Volden, 2006). Individuals, in a particular context, are able to derail the direction of monetary policy; it is not the parties (Krehbiel, 1998). To account for this, I created a dummy variable that measures the party of the chairman of the SBC (Democrat [1 = yes or 0 = no]; Republican [1 = yes or 0 = no]). Similarly, I created another dummy variable that measured the party control of the Congress by chamber (Chamber Control House—Democrat [1 = yes or 0 = no]; Republican [1 = yes or 0 = no] and Senate—Democrat [1 = yes or 0 = no]; Republican [1 = yes or 0 = no]). To better represent the effect of party on the changes in the FFR, I created two dummy variables that measure changes in party control (Change in Party Leadership [Senate—1 = yes or 0

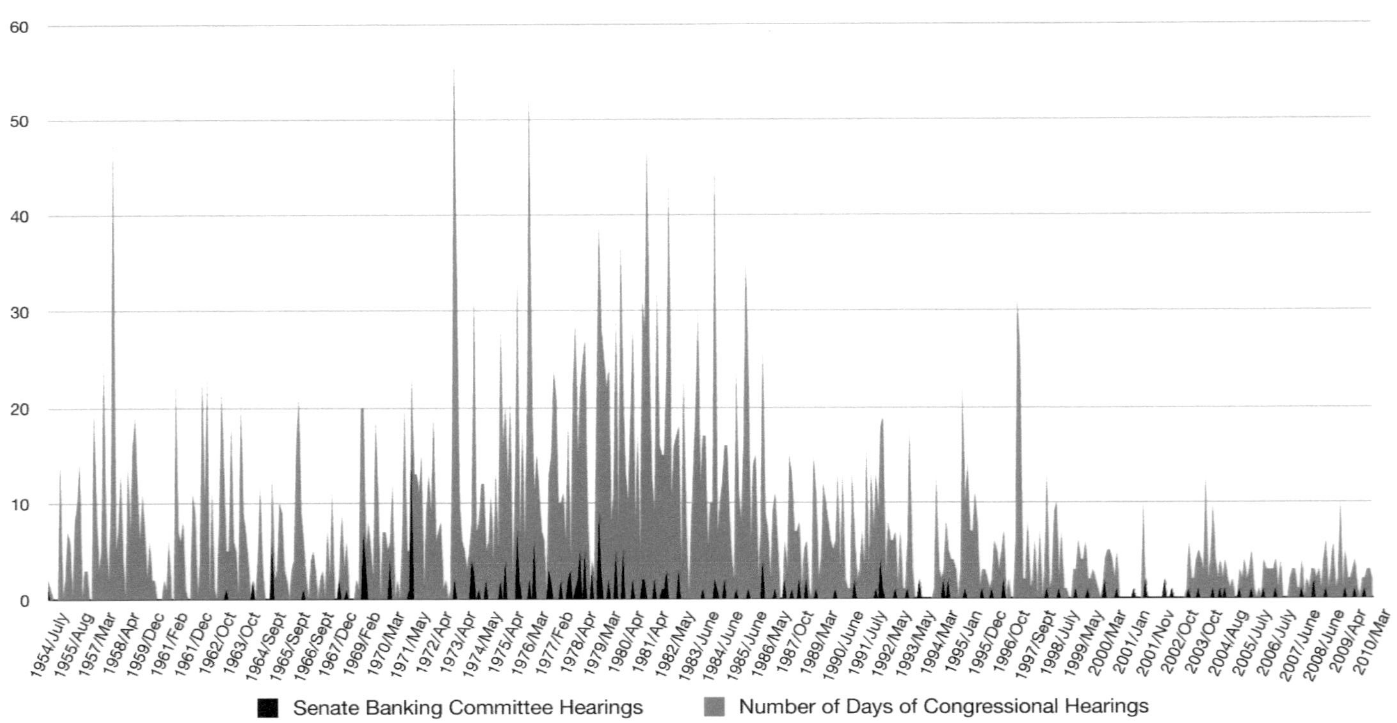

Figure 3.2. Monthly Totals of Congressional Hearings on the Economy July 1954–January 2012.
Adapted from *Policy Agendas Project*, 2014.

Table 3.4. Senate Banking Committee Chairmen Differentiated by Political Affiliation and History.

Banking Committee	*Extracted from the Biographical Directory of the U.S. Congress* — *Republican Party*	*Democratic Party*
1953–1954	Homer E. Capehart (1897–1979) Republican Party (IN) 1945–1963	
1955–1959		J. William Fulbright (1905–1995) Democratic Party (AR) 1945–1974
1959–1966		A. Willis Robertson (1887–1971) Democratic Party (VA) 1946–1966
1967–1974		John J. Sparkman (1899–1985) Democratic Party (AL) 1946–1979
1975–1980		William Proxmire (1915-2005) Democratic Party (WI) 1957–1989
1981–1986	Jake Garn (1932–) Republican Party (UT) 1974–1993	
1987–1988		William Proxmire (1915–2005) Democratic Party (WI) 1957–1989
1989–1994		Donald W. Riegle, Jr. (1938–) Democratic Party (MI) 1976–1995
1995–1998	Alfonse M. D'Amato (1937–) Republican Party (NY) 1981–1999	
1999–2001	Phil Gramm (1942–) Republican Party (TX) 1985–2002	
2001–2002		Paul S. Sarbanes (1933–) Democratic Party (MD) 1977–2007
2003–2006	Richard C. Shelby (1934–) Republican Party (AL) 1987–	
2007–2010		Christopher J. Dodd (1944–) Democratic Party (CT) 1981–2011
2011–2014		Timothy P. Johnson (1946–) Democratic Party (SD) 1997–2014

Adapted from Senate Banking Committee Official Website, 2014.

= no] and [House—1 = yes or 0 = no]). I also included a dummy variable that measured the presence of divided government (1 = president and Congress are a different party; 0 = president and Congress are same party).

Economic Indicators (M3)

There are specific economic indicators that are essential to understanding the health of the economy: unemployment rate, inflation rate, and GDP.

These data are available on the BLS. They are monthly and quarterly data. This is crucial for economic policymaking for many reasons. For the third model (M3), I coded the unemployment rate each month (3.4 to 10.8), the inflation rate each month (–2.1 to 14.8), and the quarterly GDP rate (2,332.4 to 13,506.4). Political actors, particularly presidents and members of Congress, behave differently during times of recession (Dolan, Frendreis, and Tatalovich, 2008; Hoffman and Howard, 2010; Wood, 2007). To account for this in the model, I created a dummy variable that measures the presence of a recession (1 = yes or 0 = no).

Control Variables

The seven hypotheses presented above are the primary justifications for the analysis; however, consideration of how presidential political party plays into the Fed's economic behavior, how the presidents' approval ratings play a role, and the extent to which the presidential calls for legislation affect the behavior of the Fed will also offer insight into the Fed's attention to congressional party leadership. Given the lack of previous research on these control variables, this analysis investigated the influence of presidential rhetoric, congressional attention, and economic conditions in the context of these factors.

Dependent Variable

The Fed is an independent agency that has substantive influence over monetary policy (Morris, 2000). The changes it makes to the FFR are indicative of changes in the overall economy, which is why the FFR was chosen as one measure of the economic behavior of the Fed (Beck, 1982). I obtained the FFR from the Fed's Statistical Release website from July 1954 through January 2012, as illustrated by figure 3.3. There was no reason to code the FFR as it is already presented in a time series (monthly) format. The FFR is conveyed in percentages from 0.07 to 19.1 percent each month. The rate does not change every month. There are times when the FFR is the same from month to month. The Fed Board is under no obligation to change the FFR from month to month. Changing the interest rates or keeping those rates constant is their prerogative.

Effect of Presidential Rhetoric on the Federal Funds Rate

The first model (M1) is completely in-line with the hypotheses; the positive or negative rhetoric and the control variables in this analysis do not significantly shape the Fed's decision to change the FFR consistently over time

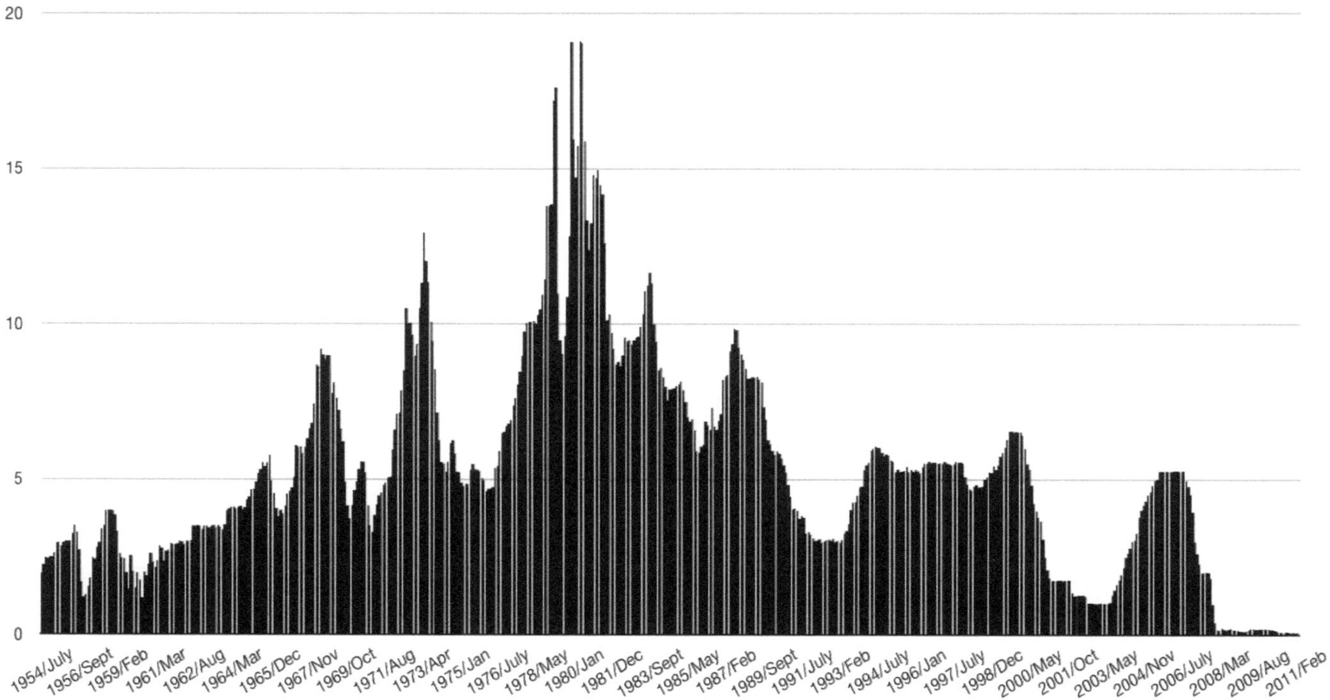

Figure 3.3. Federal Funds Rate from July 1954–January 2012.
Adapted from Federal Reserve Official Website, 2014.

and in the aggregate. Moreover, the R^2 and the adjusted R^2 values indicate that the model is seriously lacking; the use of presidential rhetoric is not a complete picture of what motivates the economic behavior of the Fed. To express this, the regression took the form

$FFR_{i,t} = \alpha + \gamma$ *Presidential Rhetoric*$_{i,t} + \hat{\beta_1}$ *Presidential Party*$_{i,t} + \hat{\beta_2}$ *Presidential Approval Rating* $+ \hat{e}_{i,t}$ (M1)

This regression enabled me to test the argument that the president's position as the foremost economic leader allows for the use of rhetoric as a mechanism of presidential power that can influence the behavior of economic actors. The specification controls for the $FFR_{i,t}$, wherein the *i* represents each individual rate determined by the Fed in each period *t* (month). Therefore, I regressed the $FFR_{i,t}$ on the rhetoric of the presidents, a vector of different expressions of presidential speeches ($\hat{\beta_1}$ *Positive Ratio*$_{i,(t-1)+(t-2)} + \hat{\beta_2}$ *Negative Ratio*$_{i,(t-1)+(t-2)} + \hat{\beta_3}$ *Number of Positive Statements*$_{i,t} + \hat{\beta_4}$ *Number of Negative Statements*$_{i,t} + \hat{\beta_5}$ *Number of Speeches*$_{i,t} + \hat{\beta_6}$ *Calls for Legislation*$_{i,t}$) as well as two control variables signifying aspects of presidential power, namely, party identification and presidential approval ratings.

Table 3.5 presents the coefficients, standard errors, semirobust standard errors,[3] and *p*-values as well as the measures of fit for the Prais-Winston Regression Analysis. In hypothesis 1, I found that the data require a rejection of the null hypothesis. It is not significantly more likely that the estimates of the ratio of positive economic rhetoric have any influence on the Fed's economic behavior with regard to the FFR. Moreover, the number of positive statements had no substantive effect on the FFR either. The data suggest that the Fed either responded to the president's positive economic rhetoric by leaving the FFR where it was or the Fed lowered it, as the alternative hypothesis stated.

The results suggest that the tone, particularly a positive tone, is not the best measure of classification for presidential rhetoric and its effect on the economic behavior of the Fed. As illustrated by figure 3.4, there are peaks of presidential positivity regarding the economy; these peaks typically correlate with times of economic prosperity, as measured by standard economic indicators of the economy's health (Dolan, Frendreis, and Tatalovich, 2008). Despite concentrated efforts by presidents to use toned rhetoric to shape behavior, the tone does not adequately engender a response to their entrepreneurial agenda. The results suggest, rather, that the Fedis responsive to other conditions more so than the notion that they are attentive to the presidential cues regarding the direction the economy should go in the future.

Table 3.5. Prais-Winston Regression Estimates of Presidential Economic Rhetoric on the FFR.

	Dependent Variable: FFR (Monthly) July 1954–January 2012 N = 568			
	(M1) Rho = 0.9829			
	Coefficients	*Standard Errors*	*Semirobust Standard Errors*	*p-Values*
Ratio Positive Statements	0.0183	0.0897	0.0650	0.839
Ratio Negative Statements	0.1838	0.1166	0.2144	0.116
Positive Lag 1	−0.0327	0.0888	0.0634	0.713
Positive Lag 2	0.0671	0.0762	0.0609	0.379
Negative Lag 1	0.1190	0.1023	0.1692	0.245
Negative Lag 2	0.0576	0.0920	0.1181	0.533
Number Positive Statements	−0.0069	0.0246	0.0171	0.779
Number Negative Statements	−0.0213	0.0382	0.0487	0.577
Number of Speeches	0.0019	0.0030	0.0031	0.531
Calls for Legislation	−0.0161	0.0302	0.0205	0.595
Presidential Approval Rating	0.0005	0.0055	0.0061	0.927
Presidential Party	−0.1659	0.2462	0.1500	0.501
F (12,555) – Statistic = 0.52 (p = 0.9024) R^2 = 0.0111				
Adjusted R^2 = −0.0103 MSE = 0.63963				

In hypothesis 2, I also found that the data require a rejection of the null hypothesis. It is not significantly more likely that the negative economic rhetoric substantively influences the Fed's economic behavior with regard to the FFR. The changes that did transpire in the FFR are statistically indecipherable from no change; it is important to note, however, that the p-value was 0.116. The data suggest that the Fed either responded to the president's aggregated, negative economic rhetoric by leaving the FFR where it was or the Fed raised the FFR, as the alternative hypothesis stated.

As illustrated by figure 3.5, the negative rhetoric encompasses only 30 percent of the total statements on the economy. The role the presidents play in economic discussions is a difficult balancing act; presidents do not want to bring too much attention to the flailing economy with their negative rhetoric. They run the risk of an electoral backlash wherein the public blames them for the state of the economy (Vavreck, 2009). This reality might somewhat factor into the presidential strategy of discussing the economy

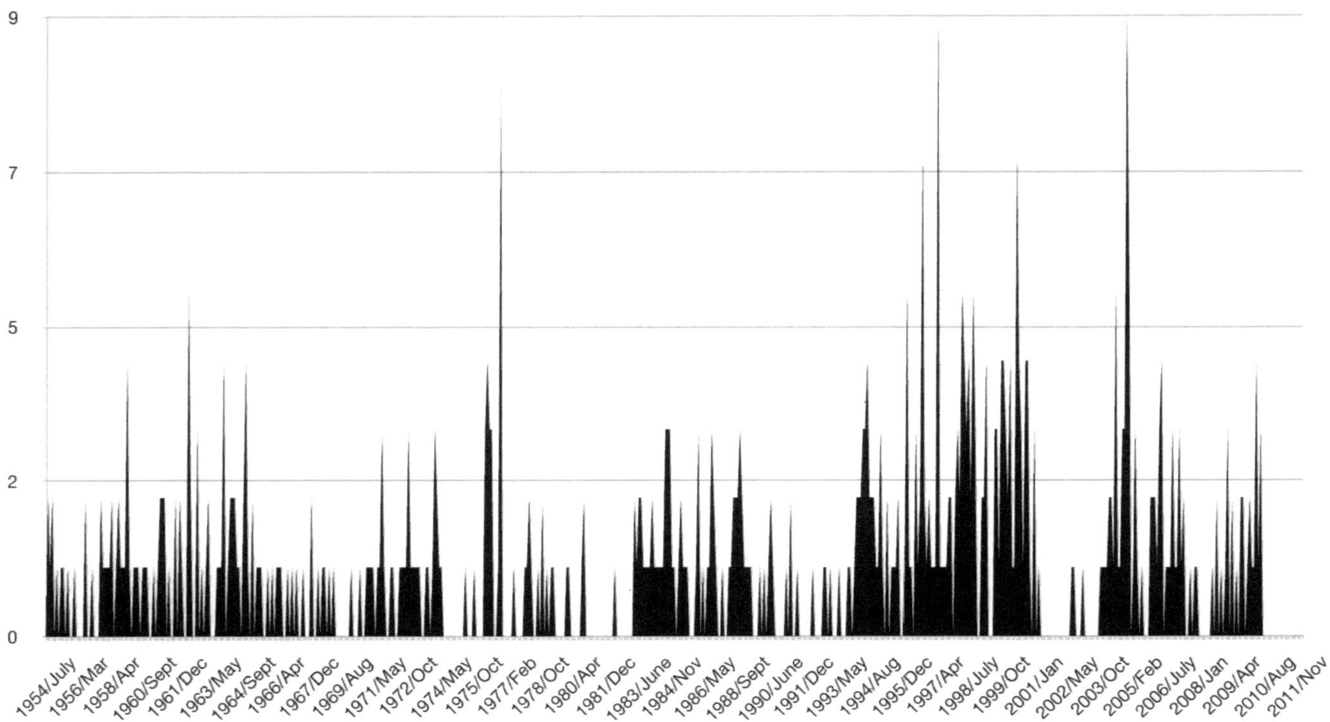

Figure 3.4. Monthly Totals of Presidential Positivity July 1954–January 2012.
Adapted from *The American Presidency Project*, 2014.

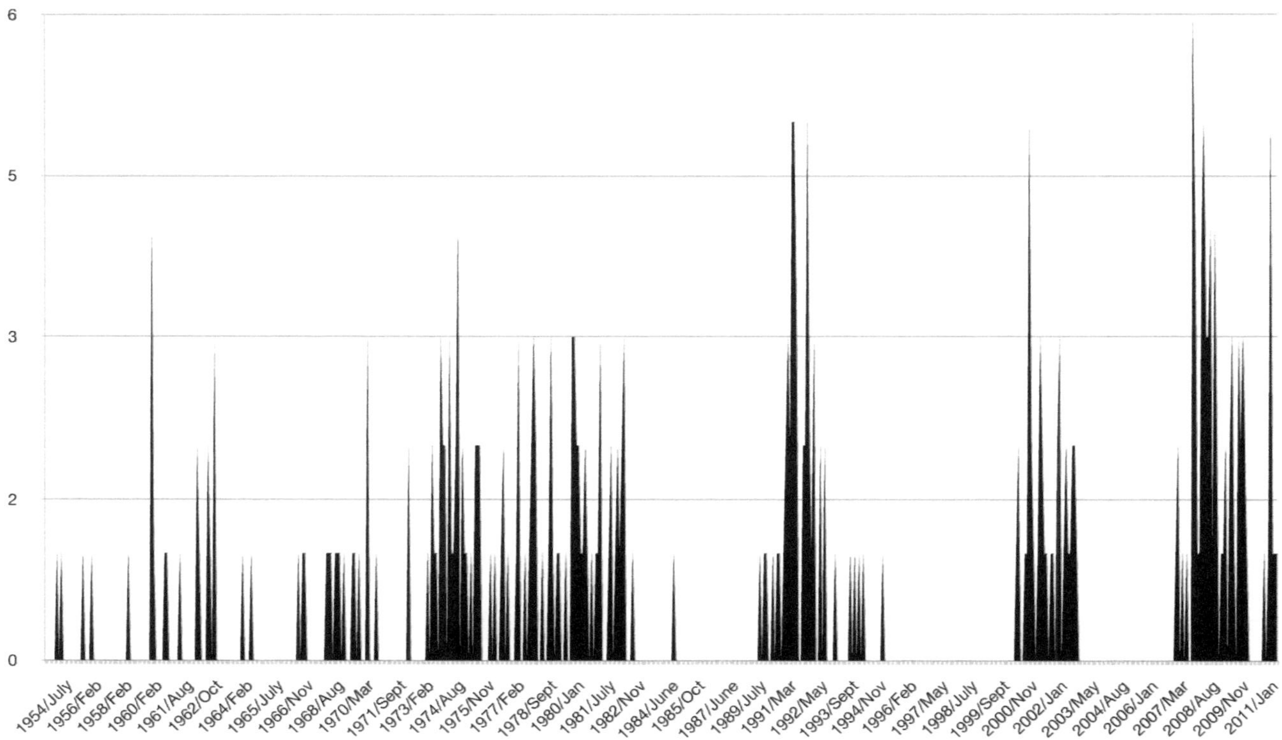

Figure 3.5. Monthly Totals of Presidential Negativity July 1954–January 2012.
Adapted from *The American Presidency Project*, 2014.

positively most of the time. Nearly 55 percent of their economic rhetoric is positive; it is a redirection of sorts (Arthur and Woods, 2013).

The data suggest that classifying presidential economic rhetoric in terms of negativity is not the most effective approach for ascertaining the influence presidents have over economic actors either; this type of rhetoric is used too infrequently to garner a significant influence. The impetus for changes in the FFR seems to be influenced by other conditions rather than toned presidential rhetoric. I must note, however, that the more negative speeches the president gives, there is about a 5 percent negative change in the FFR.

The second model (M2) is also completely in line with the hypotheses; congressional actions and party control provide an appropriate measure of influence on the changes to the FFR. To express this, the regression took the form

$$FFR_{i,t} = \alpha + \gamma\, Member\ Party\ Affiliation_{i,t} + \gamma\, Congressional\ Attention_{i,t} + \hat{\beta_1}\, Presidential\ Party_{i,t} + \hat{\beta_2}\, Divided\ Government_{i,t} + \hat{e}_{i,t}$$

This regression enabled me to test the argument that the Fed is more responsive to congressional party affiliations, party changes, and their attention to the economy rather than presidential rhetoric and influence. Again, the specification controls for the $FFR_{i,t}$, wherein the *i* represents each individual rate determined by the Fed in each period *t* (month). Again, we regress the $FFR_{i,t}$ on member party affiliations, a vector of various representations of the importance of party ($\hat{\beta_1}$ *Party Sen. Banking Committee Chair*$_{i,t}$ + $\hat{\beta_2}$ *Party Change Senate*$_{i,t}$ + $\hat{\beta_3}$ *Party Change House*$_{i,t}$ + $\hat{\beta_4}$ *Party Control House*$_{i,t}$) and another vector of congressional attention ($\hat{\beta_1}$ *Days of Congressional Hearings*$_{i,t}$ + $\hat{\beta_2}$ *Days of Senate Banking Comm. Hearings*$_{i,t}$) as well as two control variables: divided government and presidential party.

Table 3.6 presents the coefficients, standard errors, semirobust standard errors, and *p*-values as well as the measures of fit for the Prais-Winston Regression Analysis. Congressional actions and party control provide a better mechanism for assessing the economic behavior of the Fed. In hypothesis 3, the data suggest that the chairperson of the SBC has a substantive influence with the economic decision-making of the Fed. As presented by table 3.6, the Fed is significantly more likely to raise the FFR when the chairman of the SBC is a Republican, indicating that the Fed pays attention to the party ideology in Congress regarding the economy. In this instance, the Fed pursued a contractionary monetary policy (higher interest rates) more so when a Republican was the chairman of the SBC.

Table 3.6. Prais-Winston Regression Estimates of Congressional Economic Behavior on the FFR.

	Dependent Variable: FFR (Monthly) July 1954–January 2012 N = 550			
	(M2) Rho = 0.9772			
	Coefficients	*Standard Errors*	*Semirobust Standard Errors*	*p-Values*
Sen. Bank Comm. Chair Party	1.514	0.2535	0.8031*	0.0000
Days Congress Hearings	–0.0019	0.0030	0.0040	0.5280
Sen. Bank Comm. Hearings	0.0274	0.0164	0.0220	0.0960
Senate Party Change	0.9869	0.1921	0.5458*	0.0000
House Party Change	–1.521	0.3734	0.6855**	0.0000
Party Control in House	–1.504	0.5013	0.8357*	0.0030
Divided Government	0.9574	0.2072	0.4602**	0.0000
Presidential Party	0.0348	0.2420	0.2090	0.8860
F (8,541) – Statistic = 8.77 (p = 0.0000) R^2 = 0.1148 Adjusted R^2 = 0.1017 MSE = 0.61316				

*$p < 0.1$.

**$p < 0.05$.

In hypothesis 4, I measured the effect of congressional hearings in two different ways—number of days of hearings on the economy and number of days of hearings in the SBC regarding monetary policy. The statistical effect of the overall number of hearings on the economy indicates that the more hearings on the economy Congress has the more likely the Fed would *lower* the FFR; the effect, however, was not distinguishable from zero. The hearings in the SBC did have a measurable effect, however; it was only at the 0.10 alpha level. The more hearings on the economy the SBC has the more likely the Fed *raised* the FFR.

To further measure the effects of Congress on the changes in the FFR, I assessed when each chamber had a change in the majority party. As seen in table 3.6, party changes in Congress had a substantive impact on the Fed's economic behavior. For instance, when a party change occurred in the Senate, the FFR increased substantially and when a party change occurred in the House, the FFR decreased substantially. One could speculate that the Fed is aware of the significance and magnitude of a particular party going from the minority party with constrained influence to the majority party, who possesses the ability to intervene in the Fed's organization, mission, and existence. Regardless of what caused the changes in the chambers, these results suggest that the Fed responds to these changes. Moreover, as seen earlier, the Fed responds to the party ideology of the respective majority party.

The results here indicate that the Fed is attentive to Congress when considering whether to change the FFR. At the very least, the Fed considers factors such as the majority party in congressional leadership, political ideology, and political climate when choosing a particular course of action regarding monetary policy.

The third model (M3) is partly in-line with the hypotheses; the economic indicators mostly provide an appropriate estimate of the Fed's economic behavior. To express this, the regression took the form

$$FFR_{i,t} = \alpha + \gamma \, Economic\ Indicators_{i,t} + \hat{\beta_1}\, Presence\ of\ a\ Recession_{i,t} + \hat{e}_{i,t}$$

This regression enabled me to test the argument that the Fed is more responsive to the conditions related to the economy rather than presidential rhetoric and influence. Again, the specification controls for the $FFR_{i,t}$, wherein the *i* represents each individual rate determined by the Fed in each period *t* (month). Again, we regress the $FFR_{i,t}$ on the economic conditions, a vector of various economic indicators ($\hat{\beta_1}\, Unemployment\ Rate_{i,t} + \hat{\beta_2}\, Inflation\ Rate_{i,t} + \hat{\beta_3}\, Gross\ Domestic\ Product_{i,t}$) as well as a control variable, the presence of a recession. Table 3.7 presents the coefficients, standard errors, semirobust standard errors, and *p*-values as well as the measures of fit for the Prais-Winston Regression Analysis. Economic indicators provide a better indicator for changes in the FFR than presidential rhetoric does.

In hypothesis 5, I measured the effect of GDP on the FFR. The Fed raised the FFR as the GDP went down indicating that the direction in the hypothesis was correct. The result was indecipherable from zero, as was the dummy variable measuring the presence of a recession. As expected, in hypotheses 6 and 7, the unemployment rate and the inflation rate, seem to be profoundly instrumental in the Fed's decision to change the FFR, as illustrated by table 3.7. In each decision that the Fed makes, whether to raise or lower the FFR, there is a significant result for unemployment and inflation. Particularly, as the unemployment rate decreases, the Fed raises the FFR, an indicator that the economy is getting better. These data suggest that the Fed is most likely responding to the economic indicators rather than the rhetoric from the president, which makes sense given their legal obligation and concern

Table 3.7. Prais-Winston Regression Estimates of Pertinent Economic Indicators on the FFR.

	Dependent Variable: FFR (Monthly) July 1954–January 2012 N = 550			
	(M3) Rho = 0.9787			
	Coefficients	*Standard Errors*	*Semirobust Standard Errors*	*p-Values*
Unemployment Rate	–0.6450	0.1253	0.1874**	0.000
Inflation Rate	0.1836	0.0584	0.0761*	0.002
Gross Domestic Product	–0.0002	0.0003	0.0002	0.524
Recession	0.0351	0.1509	0.0984	0.816
F (4,545) – Statistic = 9.70 (p = 0.0000) R^2 = 0.0665 Adjusted R^2 = 0.0596 *MSE* = 0.6273				

*$p < 0.05$.

**$p < 0.001$.

with inflation and unemployment (Edwards and Wood, 1999). Therefore, one might speculate that if the economy is getting better, the Fed is more likely to raise the FFR as a result of those healthful indicators rather than the positive rhetoric from the president, which is most likely a result of the positive economy.

Conclusion

The Fed is responsible for regulating inflation by altering interest rates on monies loaned to banks. Their ability to change the FFR has a substantial impact on the economy (Frumkin, 2004). Because of the Fed's role in the economy, presidential administrations are highly concerned with this bureaucratic organization; the decisions the Fed employs can make the achievement of other economic policy goals difficult. Yet, there is no consensus or substantive discussion in the literature as to the ability of the president to effectively use rhetoric, cues, and signals to shape the economic behavior of one of the most substantial economic actors—the Fed. However, extent research indicates that political actors respond and produce cues as a mechanism of political behavior and persuasion (Edwards and Wood, 1999; Eshbaugh-Soha, 2006; Light, 1999; Yates and Whitford, 2005). Therefore, this analysis sought an answer as to whether presidents try to shape the Fed with rhetorical cues and the extent to which they are successful.

There is a literature that argues that presidential rhetoric is able to motivate certain economic actors by signaling their tone, their political position, and their level of commitment (Eshbaugh-Soha, 2006; Wood, 2007). However, that literature, specifically, glosses over the externalities that potentially affect the changes in the economy, the constraints of the separated system of American government, and the limitations inherent in the president's ability to use rhetoric to achieve desired results. My analysis has allowed for a more comprehensive research operationalization rather than arguing that the president's ability to change economic indicators comes from his position as the most important economic actor in the system (Eshbaugh-Soha, 2007; Wood, 2007). By expanding the data sources and the audience of pertinent economic actors, I offered a more comprehensive assessment of presidential influence with economic actors and the results suggests that previous research might not be the definitive word on the presidential influence (Wood, 2007).

These results have further contributed to the extant literature by ascertaining that the president does intend to cue or signal the Fed about which direction he wants monetary policy to go in the future. Further, it determines that the president, through the use of positive and negative economic rhetoric, is not overly successful in shaping the Fed's economic behavior, as seen in the changes to the FFR. This analysis does confirm what others have stated, namely, that presidents have increased their rhetoric on the economy significantly (Wood, 2007). However, my research suggests that the increased rhetoric and attention to the economy has not brought about the desired effects for which presidents advocate. The changes in the FFR were not statistically significant and could not be recognized from zero. Moreover, when considering the Fed's claim of independence from politics, it is unlikely that they would risk congressional intervention and changes to their organization because they did the bidding of a sitting president. Secondly, the Fed is unlikely to help a sitting president in an election year; the Fed's intervention in an election may harm the organization more so than any political capital it may gain by meddling (Beck, 1982). Therefore, it is more likely that the economic behavior of the Fed is shaped by congressional party affiliations, party changes, and their attention to the economy as well as economic indicators rather than the cues and signals the president sends to the Fed.

The results actually provided three specific components that show the extent to which the Fed pays attention to the presidents' rhetoric, congressional actions, and indicators of the economy's strength. Conducting the analysis in this manner provided a picture of how the presidents discuss the economy in their speeches, particularly with regard to the tone. These results suggest that the Fed did not respond to the rhetorical cues and signals; the rhetorical assessment of the economy does not shape how the Fed reacts to presidential assessments of the economy. The presidential rhetoric did not have a substantive effect on the raising or lowering of the FFR because of the tone within speeches (positive/negative). Such an understanding provides insight into presidential influence over economic actors and the economy; it is clear that the lack of significance in presidential rhetoric's ability to predict changes in the FFR is telling from a "rhetoric as mechanism of influence" perspective. Despite presidential attempts to tailor their rhetoric to influence specific actors, they are incredibly unsuccessful, in nearly every way.

Notes

1. Regressing the FFR on every variable in all three models was not substantively different than creating three models. It made more sense, theoretically, to differentiate the models.

2. I must attach a word of caution about some of my hypotheses. Publishing null hypotheses is difficult. However, it is not unprecedented when warranted. Many scholars have done this. Not all of the hypotheses in the entire book take the "null hypothesis" approach, however. Those that do are warranted. However, I must argue that this analysis, based upon the theory and its response to the extant literature, warrants the null hypothesis approach. Therefore, if there is no effect, I am correct; there is no consideration of the magnitude by which rhetoric affects the FFR. I was not interested in magnitude, but rather the president's ability to influence the decision-making of an economic actor with the tone present in the rhetoric. I assume that my alternative hypothesis is correct until I could find evidence that it was incorrect. No such evidence could be found in this instance. I set up the analysis this way on purpose. I know that it makes it easier to obtain and justify my results. I think that the analysis still warrants a contribution to the literature. I took multiple measures to ensure that I gave presidential rhetoric a chance to make an impact. I differentiated the rhetoric by the tone of the speech, the type of speech as well as the time period; it was not a simple aggregation of words. However, one could still read the results with caution because the rhetoric used was a stratified random sample and not the complete analysis of every word every president spoke.

3. The Semirobust Standard Errors were included in the tables to simply indicate the changes that the Cochrane–Orcutt estimation made to the standard errors in the Prais-Winston Regression Analysis. The significance of each variable was not changed substantively. However, I have indicated the changes in alpha levels, which were noteworthy.

CHAPTER FOUR

Presidential Rhetoric and Public Perceptions

Economic depression cannot be cured by legislative action or executive pronouncement. Economic wounds must be healed by the action of the cells of the economic body—the producers and consumers themselves.

—Herbert C. Hoover (Woolley and Peters, 2014 —"Herbert Hoover, 1930")

President Bush and the Economy after September 11, 2001

President Bush addressed the nation on the evening of September 11 after the terrorist attacks. He began the speech with the imagery that penetrated the American consciousness on that day: violence, death, fire, fear, and terror. Within minutes into the speech, he addresses the economy, "Our financial institutions remain strong, and the American economy will be open for business as well" (Woolley and Peters, 2014—"George Bush, September 11"). He then transitions to a discussion regarding the search for those who committed the attacks. President Bush's comment on the economy is subtle, not overbearing, and very telling; it illustrates a fundamental aspect of presidential expectations regarding the economy. Even in the midst of such tragic death and destruction, the president of the United States thought it was necessary to address the economy, envisioning the concerns people may have about its future viability.

Already in a recession, beginning in March 2001, the economy took a serious turn for the worse immediately after September 11, 2001. The recession was extended, as a result of the terror attacks, causing the economy to contract further rather than continue the slight expansion. The stock market was closed for nearly a week and upon its opening lost over six hunred points (7 percent). Persistent and perpetual discussions of war kept the market from fully rebounding for nearly a year. Despite some minor progress, it took another major decrease in March 2003. Furthermore, unemployment continued to rise after 9/11, reaching 6 percent by mid-June 2003. According to some reports, an estimated 600,000 jobs were lost as a result of 9/11 (Kiplinger, 2014). In the days after 9/11, President Bush continued to address the economic conditions:

> But we hope, obviously, that the measures we take will allow the American economy to continue on. I urge people to go to their businesses on Monday. I understand Major League Baseball is going to start playing again. It is important for America to get on about its life. (Woolley and Peters, 2014—"George Bush, September 15")

> But I have great faith in the resiliency of the economy. And no question about it, this affected our economy. But the markets open tomorrow, people go back to work, and we'll show the world. (Woolley and Peters, 2014—"George Bush, September 16")

> I understand it is tough right now. Transportation business is hurting. Obviously, the market was correcting prior to this crisis. But the underpinnings for economic growth are there. We're the greatest entrepreneurial society in the world. (Woolley and Peters, 2014—"George Bush, September 17")

> I ask your continued participation and confidence in the American economy. Terrorists attacked a symbol of American prosperity. They did not touch its source. America is successful because of the hard work and creativity and enterprise of our people. . . . We will come together to take active steps that strengthen America's economy and put our people back to work. (Woolley and Peters, 2014—"George Bush, September 20")

> Our economy has had a shock. Many workers lost their jobs this week. . . . I applaud those companies who are making extra efforts to avoid laying off workers even during difficult times. . . . Yet, for all of these challenges, the American economy is fundamentally strong. (Woolley and Peters, 2014—"George Bush, September 22")

The reality, however, is that the economy continued to worsen, even as President Bush offered hope and encouragement about the economy's recovery. Other economic indicators continued to deteriorate after the attacks. For instance, the Federal Reserve (Fed) had a Federal Funds Rate (FFR) of 6.5 percent before to the recession of 2001. As a result of the recession, the Fed began to change its monetary policy prior to 9/11; however, the Fed escalated those changes dramatically directly after 9/11 by reducing the FFR to its lowest in decades (1 percent). To compound the problem, the American airline industry lost half of its customers by the end of September (Kiplinger, 2014). In response to the continued job losses at airlines in the United States, President Bush said,

> We understand, when we get our airlines up and running, it's going to affect so much of our economy. And we jointly approved $15 billion of monies available to provide not only relief for airlines but loan guarantees for airlines, to make sure our airlines are strong and healthy in the aftermath of this national emergency. (Woolley and Peters, 2014—"George Bush, September 27")

Calling for government stimulus for the economy is not typically the economic policy of a fiscally conservative Republican president. Presidential expectations regarding the economy compelled President Bush to pursue whatever economic policy direction was the most feasible and expected by the people and the market.

Essentially, the economy was in shambles after 9/11, continuing the decline that started in March, and it perpetually got worse as the days unfolded. The uncertainty of the future festered in the public's perceptions of the economy and the vicissitudes of the markets exacerbated the situation. President Bush had an incredibly difficult task in balancing his economic leadership responsibilities—maintain an accurate depiction of the difficulties transpiring in the economy for people and businesses as well as providing hope and optimism that the economy would recover in a timely fashion, alleviating the fear and trepidation for those that participate in the market. For instance, President Bush could not even bring himself to say the word "recession" after being asked on multiple occasions. On October 2, 2001, a reporter blatantly asks the president, "Are we in a recession, sir?" President Bush responds, "Are we in a what?" The reporter repeated the question and the president responded by saying, "You let the number crunchers tell us that. But there is no question our economy is hurt as a result of September 11. . . . We don't need numbers to tell us people are hurting" (Woolley and Peters, 2014—"George Bush, October 2"). President Bush would not admit or even say the word recession until December 1 on his weekly radio program wherein he says, "the official announcement came that our economy has been in recession since March. And unfortunately, to a lot of Americans, that news comes as no surprise." (Woolley and Peters, 2014—"George Bush, December 1").

Given the prevailing theories, the environment was ripe with potential for President Bush to influence the economic actors and assert a perception of economic leadership after 9/11 that engendered change and action. After 9/11, President Bush's approval ratings rose to unprecedented numbers. The day the attacks occurred, the 51 percent of the public approved and 39 percent disapproved of his performance. As we know, this is fairly average for a first-year president. At the next incident wherein the approval was measured (September 14/15), 85 percent of the public approved and only 9 percent disapproved of his handling of his job performance. This is such a dramatic change, obviously brought about from the attacks. President Bush's approval ratings topped 89 percent and remained in the seventies until July 2002. His approval rating did not drop below 60 percent until January 2003, rising back to the low seventies and mid-sixties in March 2003 through August 2003. His approval remained in the high fifties and forties until the fall of 2005 where it began to decline rapidly (Woolley and Peters, 2014).

Moreover, for most of the time when his approval rating was so high, he had bipartisan support in the 107th Congress (2001–2003). As the majority party in the Senate fluctuated between both major parties, the House of Representatives was solidly Republican. When the 108th Congress (2003–2005) began, President Bush had a majority Republican Senate and a majority Republican House, no divided government. He enjoyed this majority in both the Senate and the House again in the 109th Congress (2005–2007); however, he lost both of these majorities badly in 110th Congress (2007–2009).

Despite all of the rhetoric, high approval ratings, and the bipartisan support he could not convince the public to spend and take risks with their money. He tried to do this many times by saying, "I think when the investors sit back and take a hard look at the fundamentals of the economy, they'll get back in the market. I think that consumers will realize life is going on. . . . We'll come out of this, and we'll come out of it strong" (Woolley and Peters, 2014—"George Bush, September 24"). Again, he would often say, "I'm confident we can work with the Congress to come up with an economic stimulus package, if need be, that will send a clear signal to the risktakers and capital formatters of our country that the Government's going to act too" (Woolley and Peters, 2014—"George Bush, September 17"). Nevertheless, President Bush was unable to persuade the companies to maintain employment. He was unable to curb the declining consumer confidence. The Fed continued to make monetary policy decisions that indicated distress in the economy. And, it took years for the stock market to rebound. The aforementioned anecdote highlights the need for further inquiry into the notion that presidential rhetoric functions as a "mechanism of influence" in economic policy discussions.

Presidents are limited in their abilities to shape the economic news, public perceptions of the economy, and the public's economic behavior. Economic perceptions are governed by events, political context, and personal predilections. In fact, research suggests, "the president has no discernible causal impact on . . . attention to the overall economy" (Eshbaugh-Soha and Peake, 2005, p. 131). Even when the presidents are disaggregated, there is no discernible influence that can be measured, overall. For instance, despite the overt optimism about the economy and the constant "American resolve" rhetoric during President George W. Bush's administration, the majority of the public did not approve of the way he handled the economy (Eshbaugh-Soha and Peake, 2005). There is no substantive support for stating that the president is able to lead the public's economic agenda (Eshbaugh-Soha and Peake, 2011).

This chapter offers a quantitative explanation of presidential rhetoric's influence with one of the most significant economic actors, the public. Can the president garner influence with the public and overcome the personal perceptions and political predilections? The findings serve to highlight the glaring flaw in the prevailing argument that presidential rhetoric matters as a "mechanism of influence"—as the public views the president's rhetoric through the ideological lenses of the political elite with which they most likely identify. The findings provide a contribution to the literature on presidential rhetoric and public perceptions of the economy, suggesting that the influence of presidential rhetoric is limited (Cohen, 2008; Edwards, 2003; Eshbaugh-Soha, 2005; Eshbaugh-Soha and Peake, 2011; Hoffman and Howard, 2010; Wood, 2004; 2007; Wood, Owens, and Durham, 2005).

Essentially, the chapter begins by explaining the limitations presidents face when using rhetoric as a mechanism of power and influence. I first consider the literature regarding the public's perceptions of presidential economic leadership. I then discuss the literature pertaining to the president's interaction with the public before moving to the literature on elite discourse and political persuasion. To support this argument, I then offer a descriptive analysis of presidential economic rhetoric over time and differentiate it by political party. In this description, I provide a discussion of the percentages of the positivity and negativity used by presidents. Statistically, I assess how the public processes political discourse, the extent to which they pay attention to political issues, and their reactions to political rhetoric. From ascertaining the overall ineffectiveness of presidential rhetoric and persuasion with the public and media, I posit a theory and empirical model that suggests the public is more responsive to political predispositions and predilections, party ideology, and current economic conditions when deciding how they view the president's handling of the economy. The findings suggest that we reevaluate the prevailing argument that states that the public models its economic behavior and confidence on the optimism present in presidential economic rhetoric.

The Public's Perceptions of Presidential Economic Leadership

Two-thirds of all U.S. economic activity is driven by personal consumption; how individuals behave economically affects the economy considerably, and presidents are aware of how important the public is to the economy.[1] Ironically, the public expects the president to make sure the economy is sound (Vavreck, 2009; Wood, 2007; Wood, Owens, and Durham, 2005). Presenting an accurate image of the economy to the public is essential for a president. If he misconstrues the condition of the economy, it damages his image as an economic leader and the public will hold him accountable (Hoffman and Howard, 2010; Wood, 2007). This makes leading the public difficult for presidents, particularly during economic downturns (Cohen and Hamman, 2003). This fact has forced presidents to increasingly take their message about the economy to the public, and to do so more often.

Typically, as the years progress, presidents increase the percentage of their economic rhetoric in relation to their overall rhetoric: HST = 13 percent, DDE =17 percent, JFK = 17 percent, LBJ = 17 percent, RMN = 15 percent, GRF = 22 percent, JEC = 17 percent, RWR = 23 percent, GHWB = 24 percent, WJC = 32 percent, GWB = 26 percent, and BHO = 41 percent (presidents are represented by their initials). Thus, presidents often try to influence the public's perceptions of the economy with their rhetoric in order to secure their own goals, as illustrated by figure 4.1 (Brody, 1991; Cohen, 2008; Edwards, 2003; Eshbaugh-Soha and Peake, 2011; Lau and Redlawsk, 2006; Lockerbie, 2008; Wolf and Holian, 2006; Vavreck, 2009; Wood, 2007; Zaller, 1992). Can the public be convinced, by presidential rhetoric, to overlook economic concerns in spite of the actual economic conditions and take economic risks? Is the president able to shape the public's perception of the economy and their behavior with positive economic rhetoric (Wood, 2007)?

Constructing an appropriate model that ascertains how the public responds to presidential rhetoric is crucial for understanding the influence presidents have over public perceptions of the economy (Wood, 2007; Wood, Owens, and Durham, 2005). Scholars have used the Consumer

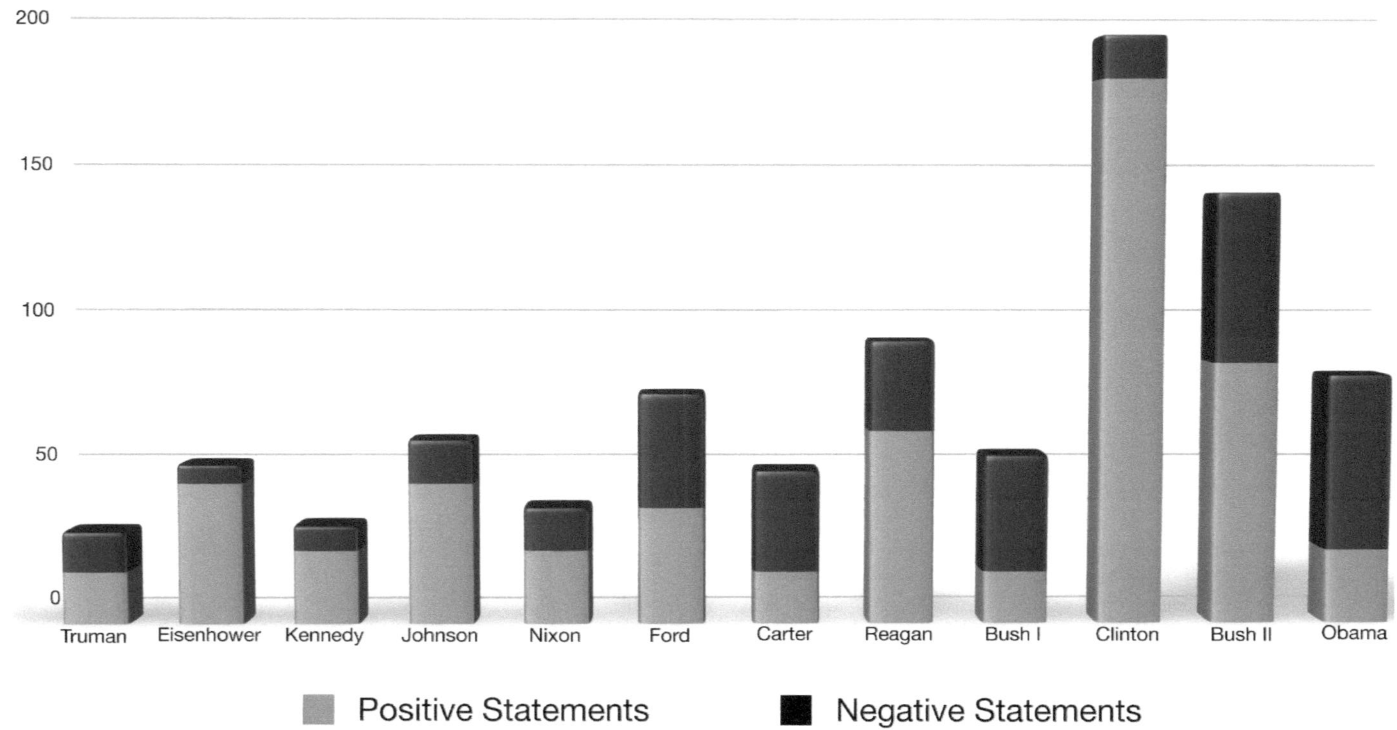

Figure 4.1. Presidential Economic Rhetoric.
Adapted from *The American Presidency Project*, 2014.

Confidence Index as a measure of how the public responds to the positive economic rhetoric (Wood, 2007; 2012).[2] Regressing the tone (positive) of presidential rhetoric on the Consumer Confidence Index does not definitively prove that the rhetoric has an influence; it does not take into account the multiple reasons for the changes in the index such as international events, whether or not they are economic in nature. There is no definitive evidence that those selected to participate in the Consumer Confidence Index survey heard the president speaking about the economy. Therefore, I am skeptical of theoretically connecting the tone of the president's rhetoric to the Consumer Confidence Index, since presidents do not have any direct connection to it, and then considering it a definitive measure of the effectiveness of presidential rhetoric. The justification for maintaining that positive gains in this *one* indicator, as somehow a definitive measure of presidential rhetoric's effect, does not provide a comprehensive assessment of the relationship between rhetoric and the public's economic behavior; thus, it does not withstand scrutiny.

An indicator of how the public perceives the president and his handling of the economy would offer a more comprehensive measure of whether he can influence the public's economic perceptions and behavior with his rhetoric. Therefore, I use the National Election Studies[3] (NES) data to assess the influence the presidents have over how the public perceives the handling of the economy.[4] These data show how the public perceives their own past, present, and future economic situations in relation to the president's attempts to shape, with the use of positive statements, the public's perceptions of the economy. Moreover, they allow for another measure of rhetoric's effect, which contributes to the large questions regarding why presidents utilize so much of their rhetorical resources on economic discussions and the extent to which they are effective.

This chapter posits that the president's relationship with the public is constrained by the limitations of audience, political predilections, and the ideological values exhibited by political parties. As a result, the economic rhetoric from the president is unable to influence or shape the public's perceptions regarding the economy; the rhetoric is not able to predict that the public will perceive the economy as "good." In fact, party identification will make more of a difference in how the public views the economy than the tone of presidential rhetoric. For instance, the public receives its information from party elites and approves or disapproves of it based upon the "elite" providing the message, complicating the president's ability to lead the public (DiClerico, 1993; Wolf and Holian, 2006). In other words, those persons who self-identify with the Democratic Party values will be more susceptible to rhetoric from Democratic presidents, although it is still not a guarantee that their will be agreement. This argument offers a more comprehensive assessment of presidential economic rhetoric literature, rather than assessing whether the president can use positive, optimistic rhetoric to shape how the overall public perceives their economic conditions (Eshbaugh-Soha, 2006; Wood, 2007; 2012; Wood, Owens, and Durham, 2005).

The President and the Public

There exists an assumption that the president has a large audience of persons who listen to what he says about any given topic (Welch, 2003). The truth, however, is that the president struggles to obtain the time, television networks, and audience necessary to sway the public. Moreover, he is not able to keep the attention of those who do actually listen. In fact, "households that watched [the major news networks], ABC, CBS, and/or NBC, declined from about 60 percent across the 1960s to 30 percent by the late 1990s" (Cohen, 2008, p. 14). The economic pressures of "ratings" forced the news media to compete for ratings with completely different shows, ones that offer entertainment rather than news; this changes the content of the news messages and the way the news media covers the president (p. 60). There are fewer and fewer persons listening to what the presidents are saying via typical media outlets such as television and radio (Barabas, 2008). Audiences are more diverse in their "news" consumption with the onset of the Internet and social media websites like Facebook and Twitter. Since the 1980s, presidents have struggled to gain audiences that even remotely approach 50 percent of viewers (Young and Perkins, 2005).[5]

Cable television ended the president's domination of the airwaves (Baum and Kernell, 1999). For decades, presidents were able to take control of prime-time moments to convey their message to those watching. With cable, however, the situation for presidents has changed. Interestingly, the impetus for the demise of presidential prime-time politics is not political dissatisfaction, but rather cable (Baum and Kernell, 1999). This is consequentially important for the presidents trying to reach a national audience by which to cue/signal, prime, or convince the public to approve of their policies; mainly because his access to the large, national audiences is diminishing. The longer the president is in office, the smaller his television audience gets (Eshbaugh-Soha and Peake, 2011).

Moreover, the news coverage of presidents has grown increasingly negative over the years, despite presidential attempts to influence the media's coverage of their actions (Cohen, 2008). In fact, from 1949 through the 1980s, the negative presidential news coverage went from 12 percent of stories to 28 percent of stories. For each individual president, the percentage of negative news increases every year the president is in office, especially after the one hundred-day honeymoon that most presidents enjoy (Cohen, 2008).

The problem is further complicated by the fact that those who do listen are not able to remember what the president said in any substantive capacity over time and across different speeches (Welch, 2003). Presidents are not able to effectively convey their message to a stable audience consistently. The media does not portray the president positively; their accomplishments are minimized, and their attempts at policy leadership are undermined by stories of personal and inconsequential anecdotes. The public is more concerned with "human interest" stories about the public, which is why the media has increased these types of stories (Cohen, 2008, p. 111). The changed media, the disconnected and truly uninformed public, and the negativity, all contribute to the president's diminished capacity to lead the public. Therefore, leading the public through positive rhetoric seems like a viable option only in years past (Eshbaugh-Soha and Peake, 2006).

The News Media and the President

In order to lead the public economically, the president needs to get his economic message to them (Cohen, 2008). Using the media is a common way for the president to reach large audiences with his message. As simple as this sounds, it is anything but simple, as discussed earlier (Baum and Kernell, 1999). The president must walk a tightrope when discussing the economy and attempting to get the media to cover the message he wants to convey to the public. The media has its own agenda and audience demands; they may not cover the economic indicators that the president has discussed. For instance, if unemployment has dropped and the president highlights this reality, the media may only discuss how low the Consumer Confidence Index has fallen. Moreover, they may cover those indicators that the president wants covered, but they may not convey the tone that the president wishes.

Constructing too dramatic a picture of the economy can have seriously negative effects for the president. Presenting the economy as better than it actually is, or ignoring the realities, makes the president seem out of touch or incompetent, both of which can be detrimental to his interaction with important actors or the electorate (Hoffman and Howard, 2010). Presidents are careful when discussing the economy to avoid drawing the media's attention to the bad economic conditions, over which they have limited control. Presidents already have a difficult time influencing what the media discusses when the economy is good; presidential interaction with the media is more confounded with a negative economy (Eshbaugh-Soha and Peake, 2005).

The media seek out negative stories about the president to increase their ratings; they are not typically trying to help the president frame the policy discussion; nor are they trying to help his reelection efforts (Eshbaugh-Soha, 2010).

The media can substantively influence the public's perception of the president; it is highly important to him, particularly because he needs them to convey his message (Eshbaugh-Soha and Peake, 2008). Despite the fact that the president is equipped with a highly functional, specialized staff that is devoted to propagandizing his message to the public and has nearly unlimited resources to travel across the country and the world to bring his message to various local constituencies, the public chooses its news outlets as a way to get information from those political elites that will confirm and reinforce their existing political predilections (Brody, 1991; Cohen, 2010; Eshbaugh-Soha and Peake, 2006). So, even though the president's cabinet level officials, political appointees, and other various supporters are, essentially, an army of presidential propaganda that floods the "talking-heads" shows and any other media outlet that will listen, the public still judges the president on those issues that *their* media makes important (Iyengar and Kinder, 1987; Page, Shapiro, and Dempsey, 1987).

The talk shows, talk radio, and programming, which focuses their coverage of political issues to coincide with the political ideologies of the audiences, has made the news more partisan (Cohen, 2008). Such media programming reinforces political ideologies and justifies resistance to political information that is contrary to held predilections (Groeling, 2008). Individuals are able to completely dismiss condemnatory information toward a president when they perceive that information as biased (Barabas, 2008; Baum and Groeling, 2008). However, when the political messages paint a propitious picture of the president whom they favor, they see the biased information as trustworthy. Individuals take information they receive and overly interpret it to fit that which supports or confirms the opinions they already hold (Chong, 1996).

The news environment that presidents face has changed dramatically and is still changing, which creates a particularly difficult challenge for presidents who choose to lead the mass public (Cohen, 2004). The tone of the local coverage of presidents in local newspapers is more negative than positive (Eshbaugh-Soha, 2010). Using different media outlets to obtain news fragments the audience; each media outlet provides its own commentary on presidential messages, thus removing the objectivity of the coverage and reinforcing the partisan approach to presidential messages; this creates a "more sensational" element to the news that caters to and solidifies the predispositions about political information that the public holds (Cohen, 2004,

p. 503). In fact, Zaller (1996) argues that, "the overall effect of habitual news reception for a case in which the media carry a steady stream of ideologically balanced communication is to drive liberals and conservatives into increasingly polarized opposition to one another" (p. 54).

Political Persuasion, Political Predilections, and Predispositions of the Public

Politics, at its core, is about persuading the public (Mutz, Sniderman, and Brody, 1996). More specifically, it is about succeeding in convincing the citizenry to change their minds and favor that which they did not favor. The reality, however, is that political persuasion in the form of individual speeches is not highly effective at convincing the public to change their minds or to think a specific way about a politically salient issue (Edwards, 2003; Mutz, Sniderman, and Brody, 1996; Zarefsky, 2004;). Presidential rhetoric cannot convince the public to think differently about political values (Doherty, 2008; Jarvis and Jones, 2005). The messages of political elites do not change the minds of those who are not predisposed to the values within the message. For instance, Republican politicians use their rhetoric to promote the Republican Party values, as do the Democrats, who use their rhetoric to advocate for Democratic Party values. The public's desire or motivation to seek out information contrary to that which they are given by the political elite is limited, which limits their political knowledge and political learning (Carpini and Keeter, 1996). If an individual is a Republican, that individual will typically assent to Republican Party ideology without any thought as to what the Democrats are advocating, even if that individual would agree with the Democrat (Vavreck, 2009). The public has already constructed their ideas about politics according to their predispositions and their attentiveness, which have developed over time and through the consistent encounters with their trusted sources of political information (Wolf and Holian, 2006).

Individuals use party identification as a way to shorten and simplify the information they have to process; it enables them to figure out the trusted sources of information (Lau and Redlawsk, 2006). Because of psychological predilections about the party identification, the public attributes certain "brands" to each party that enable them to simplify decisions about which issues gain their assent (Brody, 1991). Political information, over time, is typically consistent (Zaller, 1996). The messages from both sides of a political argument do not vary or change on major political issues. In fact, party identification is the most important element in political decision-making (Vavreck, 2009).

The predilections the public has about specific political issues provide substantive resistance to new information or opinions that differ from the prior attitude held by the public (Wolf and Holian, 2006). Individuals arrive at these beliefs "through discussion [with same-party persons], personal experience[s], and the media [that portrays their party values]" (Chong, 1996, p. 195). They use these political predispositions to accept or reject new political ideas that are contrary to those predilections. Zaller (1992) argues that, "Democrats and Republicans tend to reject messages from the opposing party, and liberals and conservatives reject persuasive communications that are inconsistent with their ideologies" (p. 267).

Despite this, presidents continue to appeal to their "party base, interest groups, and opinion[s] in localities" as a mechanism of shaping the public's perceptions; they rally their base and neglect the moderates (Cohen, 2010, p. 4). Such actions polarize political rhetoric; it is the very impetus that creates such "polarization in the political system" (Cohen, 2004, p. 493). The polarized rhetoric creates difficulty for the presidents to lead the public effectively; it reinforces the fact that the public receives its information from party elites and approves or disapproves based upon the "elite" providing the message (DiClerico, 1993; Wolf and Holian, 2006).

Political Elites and the Public

Prominent "values" are the key element to ascertaining why individuals resist certain political messages (Zaller, 1991). Individuals do not critically rationalize their values against the political messages they hear to make sure that both are compatible, but rather pay attention to party elites with similar ideologies that provide commentary on presidential actions or policies (Converse, 1964). An individual's exposure to only one source of information, information that already coincides with one's predispositions, confirms those predispositions and solidifies, in the individual's mind, the validity of that source of information. The public trusts "politically sophisticated" elites and their ideas about presidents or their policies instead of processing the information or facts themselves.

The public attributes credibility to political experts as having experience by which they can assert their opinions and ideologies; and thus can use the elites as a source of "facts" for their own political decision-making (Page, Shapiro, and Dempsey, 1987). The credibility that individuals attribute to elite political figures stems from the association that the individual feels with the political figure due to their shared "common interests" (Baum and Groeling, 2005, p. 54). Party partisanship is conspicuous when considering credibility with Republicans favoring Republican messages from Republican elites and Democrats favoring Democratic messages from Democratic elites; individuals are more likely to accept a political message from the *party* whose ideologies most closely align with their own values. This is true despite those who pay more attention to politics; even though they have more access to new political information, it is not likely that they will change their minds about an issue when encountering new information.

For instance, a split-ballot study showed that respondents were more likely to support a policy they would otherwise disagree with if they were told that Nixon was in favor of the policy (Rosen, 1973). There are other studies that have been conducted that showed similar results but with different presidents (Thomas and Sigelman, 1985). Another study went a bit further, and found that fictitious policies that were supported by the public could lose that support if people were told that the policies were from a president of a different party than they were (Mondak, 1993). Similarly, Hurwtiz (1989) found that 30 percent of participants changed their positions, when given the chance, on a policy opinion which they were told President Reagan differed with them. Party partisanship is prominent in how the public views the president (Zaller, 1987). For instance, the economic indicators, in 1982, showed positive changes in the overall economy. Those who identified as liberal believed that this economic news was biased and not true. Conservatives, however, understood the economic message to consist of validation for President Reagan's economic agenda.

Hypotheses for Predicting Changes in the Public's Perception of Economic Leadership

Assessing the president's influence with the economy and how the public perceives the president's relationship with the economy using the NES data provides a more comprehensive assessment of rhetoric's effect. It is reasonable to assume that those participating in the NES have, at the very least, a political connection between their ideas of the economy and those of the president, given the context of, and questions on, the survey. One can infer that the context of a survey dealing with politics and the public compels the participant to cognitively associate the economy and the president.

This analysis provides two specific components that will show to what extent and the manner in which the presidents pay attention to indicators of the economy's strength or weakness and, correspondingly, how the public perceives the economy as presented by the president. Moreover, it shows whether or not the president's rhetorical assessments of the economy shape the assessments of how the public reacts to his assessment of the economy.

The public is concerned and informed about the economic issues that impact their lives, particularly their economic lives (Lockerbie, 2008). The concern with their own economic well-being typically creates two types of assenter. The retrospective assenter will evaluate what has transpired during the administration and ask if they are better off now because of actions from the current president. Such an internal inspection will provide them with the information they need to decide if they are going to support the current candidate. The prospective assenter ascertains which candidate will provide the most benefits to them in the future; it is a form of cost benefit analysis. The assenter determines which candidate will enable them to be better off financially in the coming years (Lockerbie, 2008).

The predispositions the public has about which party is better able to offer economic security to them in the future often determines for which candidate (Republican or Democrat) that person will vote, offer their support, or rate highly based upon their economic leadership (Lockerbie, 2008). Studies have found that the probability of the public stating that President Reagan's handling of the economy was good increased the more conservative or Republican they were (Mondak, Mutz, and Huckfeldt, 1996). The inverse was also true. Democrats disapproved of his handling of the economy.

Moreover, those persons with similar economic circumstances typically resonate with the ideas of those presidents that offer messages that impact their own economic predicaments (Brody, 1991). In other words, those affected by unemployment will respond positively to the president who advocates for a lower unemployment. On the other hand, those that are more concerned with inflation will respond to the president's messages and policies that attempt or succeed at lowering inflation.

Based upon the external political realities of the president's relationship with the public and his inability to convince the public to view an issue a certain way, it is argued that the perceptions the public has about the economy do not reflect the tone of presidential economic rhetoric (Edwards, 2003). The expectation is that other externalities such as respondent party affiliation, media exposure, or political information as well as specific voter preferences and perceptions are better able to predict how the public views their current economic situation and their perception of the future economy.

> H1: When the respondent's attention to politics increases, it makes a significant difference in the public's perception of the president's handling of the economy.

> H2: Positive economic rhetoric creates a significant difference in the overall public's perception of the economy as good.

H3: Positive economic rhetoric from Democratic presidents creates a significant difference in the public's perception of the economy, if they are Democrats.

H4: Positive economic rhetoric from Republican presidents creates a significant difference in the public's perception of the economy, if they are Republicans.

H5: The NES respondent's views on the president's performance as president makes a significant difference in the perception of the president's handling of the economy.

H6: If NES respondent voted for the incumbent president, it makes a significant difference in their perception of the president's handling of the economy.

H7: The amount of the vote-share that the president received in the previous election makes a significant difference in the public's perception of the president's handling of the economy.

Empirical Design

Using *The American Presidency Project* data, I analyzed the presidential rhetoric from 1948 through 2008[6] to ascertain how presidents talk about the economy (see figure 4.2). I aggregated the data into the *four-year election cycle* as the unit of analysis. I merged these data with those from the NES.[7] From the hypotheses above, I determined that three separate models (M1 = the public's perception of their personal finances in the last year, M2 = the public's perception of the economy in the last year, and M3 = the public's perception of the economy in the upcoming year) were necessary to determine if presidential rhetoric was able to influence the public's economic perceptions. This provides a unique addition to the literature on presidential rhetoric by comparing how the public views the economy with how the presidents have been talking about the economy. Connecting these data offer insight into the president's ability to shape public perceptions of the economy.

Statistical Method

The analysis required an Ordered Logistic Regression to determine the effect that the independent variables can have on the predicted probability that the respondents will choose one Likert-type scale answer over the other, as illustrated by tables 4.2 through 4.5. These regression analyses use a Maximum Likelihood Estimator, an iterative method that measures the effect of

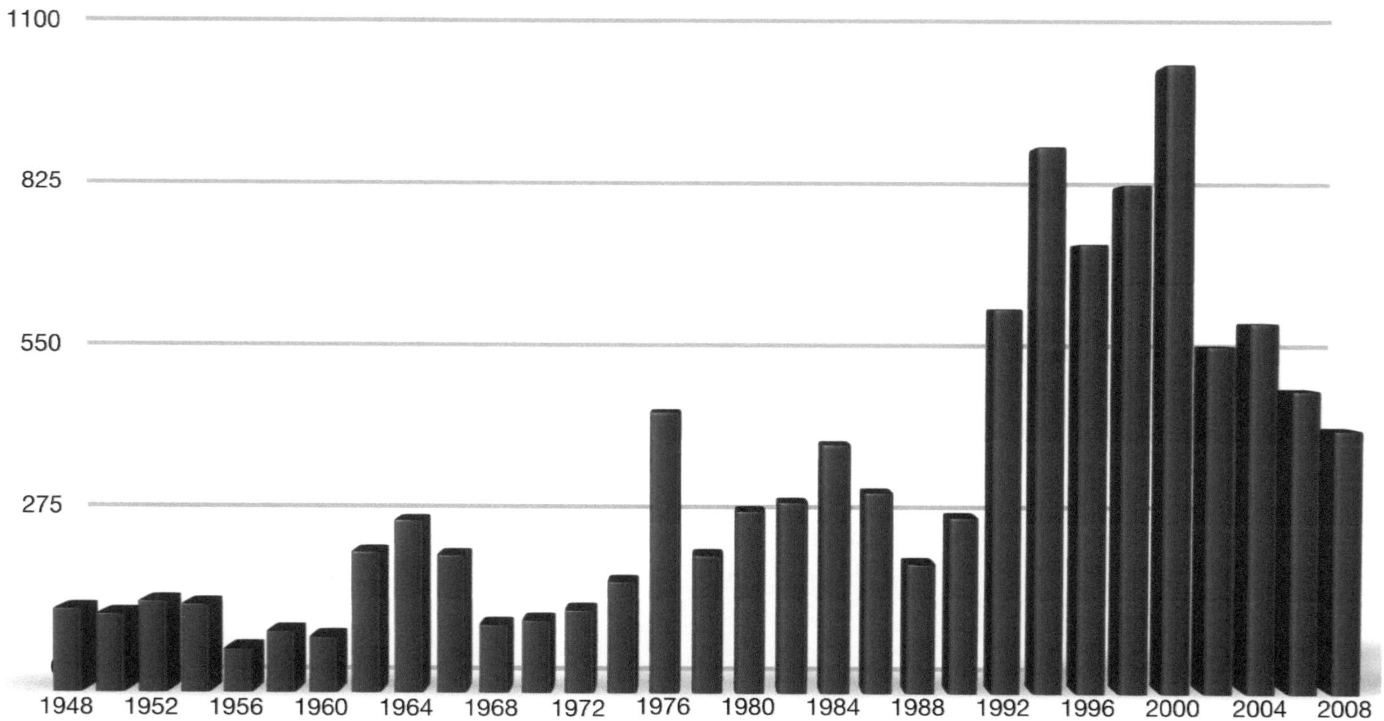

Figure 4.2. Presidential Economic Rhetoric in the Four-Year Election Cycle.
Adapted from *The American Presidency Project*, 2014.

the president's rhetoric on the public's perceptions of the economy (EP); the regression took the form

$$PR\ (EP_{i,t} = -1, 0, 1) = \alpha + \hat{\beta_1}\ \textit{Level Political Information} + \gamma\ \textit{Presidential Rhetoric}_{i,t} + \gamma\ \textit{Party Affiliation}_{i,t} + \gamma\ \textit{Economic Indicators}_{i,t} + \gamma\ \textit{Presidential Influence}_{i,t} + \hat{e}_{i,t}$$

(M1, M2, M3)

This regression enabled me to test if political party affiliations or positive economic rhetoric is better able to predict the economic perceptions of the public. The specification controls for the $EP_{i,t}$, wherein the *i* represents each individual response (–1 = Worse or 0 = Same or 1 = Better) available to the NES respondents in each period *t* (four-year election cycle). Therefore, I regress the $EP_{i,t}$ on the respondents' level of political information, the rhetoric of the presidents—a vector of different expressions of their speeches ($\hat{\beta_1}$ *Positive Ratio*$_{i,t}$ + $\hat{\beta_2}$ *Major Speeches*$_{i,t}$), party affiliations—a vector of various representations of the importance of party ($\hat{\beta_1}$ *Presidential Party*$_{i,t}$ + $\hat{\beta_2}$ *Respondent Party ID*$_{i,t}$ + $\hat{\beta_3}$ *Shared Party ID w/President*$_{i,t}$), economic indicators—a vector of different expressions of the strength of the extant economy ($\hat{\beta_1}$ *Unemployment Rate*$_{i,t}$ + $\hat{\beta_2}$ *Inflation Rate*$_{i,t}$ + $\hat{\beta_3}$ *Recession*$_{i,t}$), presidential influence indicators—a vector of different expressions of the president's influence with the public ($\hat{\beta_1}$ *Vote Share*$_{i,t}$ + $\hat{\beta_2}$ *Voting for Incumbent President*$_{i,t}$ + $\hat{\beta_3}$ Presidential Performance$_{i,t}$) as well as a control variable signifying control of government.

The ordered logistic regression provides the predicted probabilities of a one unit change in the presence of the dependent variables, *Voter Perception of the Economy in the Last Year*, the *Voter Perception of the Personal Finances in the Last Year*, and the *Voter Perception of the Economy in the Upcoming Year* (–1 = Worse, 0 = Same, 1 = Better), in this analysis of 8,829, 10,651, and 10,206 units of analysis, respectively. The log likelihood chi-squared values for the ordered logistic regression, *Voter Perception of the Economy in the Last Year* variable (5,189.25), the *Voter Perception of the Personal Finances in the Last Year* variable (931.78), and the *Voter Perception of the Economy in the Upcoming Year* variable (249.12), were all significant at the 0.0000 alpha level (see tables 4.2–4.4). Additionally, the log likelihood chi-squared values suggest that it is highly significant that the model I have created works better than one with no predictors. The model, overall, is in line with the hypotheses; the predictor variables in this analysis do significantly affect how the *public* perceives the economy as a result of the positivity and/or negativity in the president's economic rhetoric. However, as theorized, the results suggest that public perceptions of the economy are a result of party values and ideologies rather than presidential rhetoric.

Independent Variables

Identifying the presidential rhetoric aimed at the public was, again, accomplished by using the digital *Public Papers of the President* in *The American Presidency Project* from 1948 through 2008. I coded and analyzed a total of 1,524 presidential speeches. As illustrated by table 4.1, this analysis is primarily concerned with the tone (positivity, negativity) of presidential rhetoric; assessing rhetoric as political phenomena is commonly measured this way in political science literature (Arthur and Woods, 2013; Woods, 2007; Eshbaugh-Soha, 2006; Baumgartner and Jones, 2009). Each presidential mention of the economy signaling the public was coded with nine variables. Each variable was coded according to the following rubric. However, during the analysis, each categorical variable was recoded into a dummy variable so that the regressions were specified correctly.

- The ratio of positive speeches to negative and neutral speeches: (positive ratio [(positive speeches)/(positive speeches + negative speeches + neutral speeches)])
- Presidential party: Democrat (1 = yes or 0 = no); Republican (1 = yes or 0 = no)
- The inflation rate each month: (averaged for election cycle)
- Whether or not there was divided government: (1 = yes or 0 = no)
- The unemployment rate: (each month averaged for election cycle)
- The vote-share of the president: (0 to 61.1)
- Whether or not it was a major speech: (1 = yes or 0 = no)
- Whether or not there was a recession: (1 = yes; 0 = no)
- The party identification of the respondent: (0 = strong Republican; 1 = weak Republican; 2 = Independent leaning Republican; 3 = pure Independent; 4 = Independent leaning Democrat; 5 = weak Democrat; 6 = strong Democrat)
- The degree to which the respondent shared their party identification with the incumbent president: (–3 = strong Democrat; –2 = weak Democrat; –1 = Independent leaning Democrat; 0 = pure Independent; 1 = Independent leaning Republican; 2 = weak Republican; 3 = strong Republican)
- Whether or not the respondent voted for the incumbent president: (1 = yes or 0 = no)
- The respondents' perception of the presidents' performance: (1 = approve; 0 = disapprove)
- The respondents' level of political information: (1 = very low; 2 = fairly low; 3 = average; 4 = fairly high; 5 = very high)

Table 4.1. Example Sentences Measuring the Positivity of Presidential Economic Rhetoric.

D. D. Eisenhower 1/10/1960	Our economy is strong, expanding, and fundamentally sound.
L. B. Johnson 10/22/1965	We take justifiable pride in our growing national economy and in the ever-higher living standards being achieved by most Americans.
R. M. Nixon 8/15/1971	The tax reductions I am recommending, together with this broad upturn of the economy which has taken place in the first half of this year, will move us strongly forward toward a goal this nation has not reached since 1956, fifteen years ago: prosperity with full employment in peacetime.
J. E. Carter 1/06/1978	Our economy is prosperous and growing, continuing its steady recovery. Because we have confidence in the fundamental strength of our economy, we have confidence in the fundamental strength of the dollar, now and for the future.
R. W. Reagan 1/11/1986	The economy is in better shape today because we've worked hard to get the federal government out of your pockets and off your backs. We've cut taxes, limited government regulation, supported sound monetary growth, and taken commonsense steps like deregulating the price of oil.
G. H. W. Bush 6/12/1990	And what's scaring the heck out of our opponents is the simple fact that this fall they're up against the Republican record: the longest peacetime economic expansion in the history of the United States, the lowest unemployment rate in sixteen years, and almost 22 million jobs created. And Republicans are the ones who want to keep this economy strong, and we fought every step of the way against those who want to bring America to a grinding halt. . . . We're fighting against mindless redtape, more tax-and-spend programs. And we are the ones who support a balanced budget amendment and, certainly, the line-item veto because with a more sane budget process, we know that we can build a better America.
W. J. Clinton 1/6/1995	This morning I am pleased to announce that the recovery of which our economic plan was such a large part has brought paychecks to more than a quarter million more Americans in December alone. And compared with an unemployment rate of over 7 percent when I took office, we now see an unemployment rate in December of 5.4 percent. We have grown the private economy as we have cut government. That's a real recovery and a real bargain for the American people.
G. W. Bush 7/19/2008	Despite the challenges we have faced, our economy has demonstrated remarkable resilience. Exports have continued to grow; productivity growth has remained strong; and while economic growth in the first quarter of this year was slower than we would have liked, it was growth nonetheless.

Extracted from a Stratified Random Sample from the Speeches in *The American Presidency Project*

Adapted from *The American Presidency Project*, 2014.

Dependent Variables

I analyzed the NES data from 1948 through 2008 to ascertain how the public thinks about the president and his relationship with the economy.[8] The NES uses a multivariable survey with a *Likert-type* scale to determine responses from the public's opinions on political issues. I identified the most pertinent variables in the cumulative NES data set. I generated new variables that were more appropriate for ordered logistic regression analysis. The dependent variables were chosen because of their theoretical significance. This enabled me to create a set of variables that provide an original analysis of the president's influence upon voter perceptions of the economy. Connecting this information with presidential rhetoric about the economic health of the United States offers insight into the president's ability to shape public perceptions of the economy. Each NES dependent variable needed recoding in order for the analysis to work effectively:

- The voters' personal finances compared to last year: (–1 = worse; 0 = same; 1 = better)
- The voters' perception of the overall economy in the last year: (–1 = worse; 0 = same; 1 = better)
- The voters' perception of the overall economy in the upcoming year: (–1 = worse; 0 = same; 1 = better)

Descriptive Discussion

As illustrated by figure 4.3, the Republican presidents, from 1948 through 2008, used 270 *positive economic statements*, which is about 48 percent of the total positive economic statements. The Democratic presidents used 284 positive economic statements, 52 percent of the total statements. The Republican presidents used 186 *negative economic statements*, which is about 71 percent of the total negative economic statements.

As illustrated by figure 4.4, the Democratic presidents used seventy-five negative economic statements, 29 percent of the total statements. The substantial difference in presidential negative statements between Republican and Democratic rhetoric is noteworthy. I would speculate that this major discrepancy is attributed to the overwhelming fact that President Clinton spoke more often about the economy than any other president. His rhetoric was overwhelmingly positive (51 percent), which, most likely, biases this percentage. The Republican presidents used 349 *neutral economic statements*, which is about 50 percent of the total positive economic statements. The

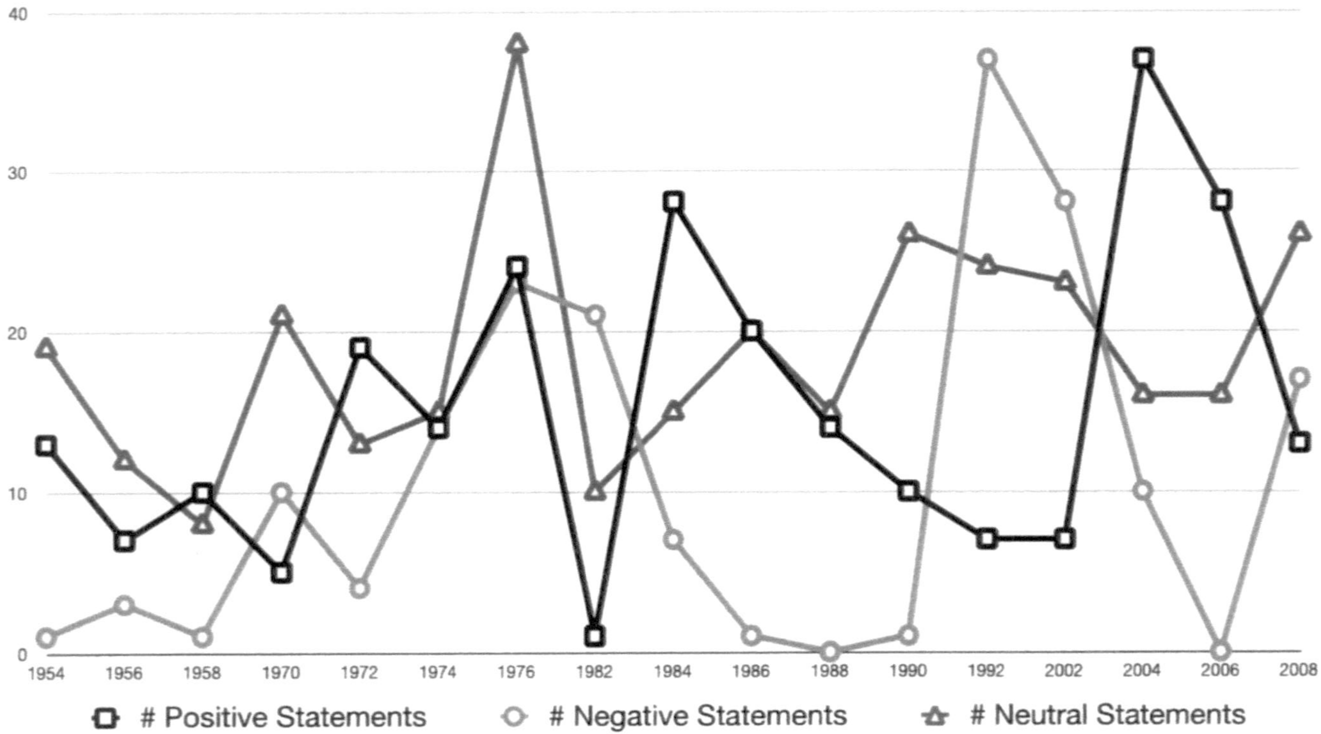

Figure 4.3. Republican Presidential Economic Statements.
Adapted from *The American Presidency Project*, 2014.

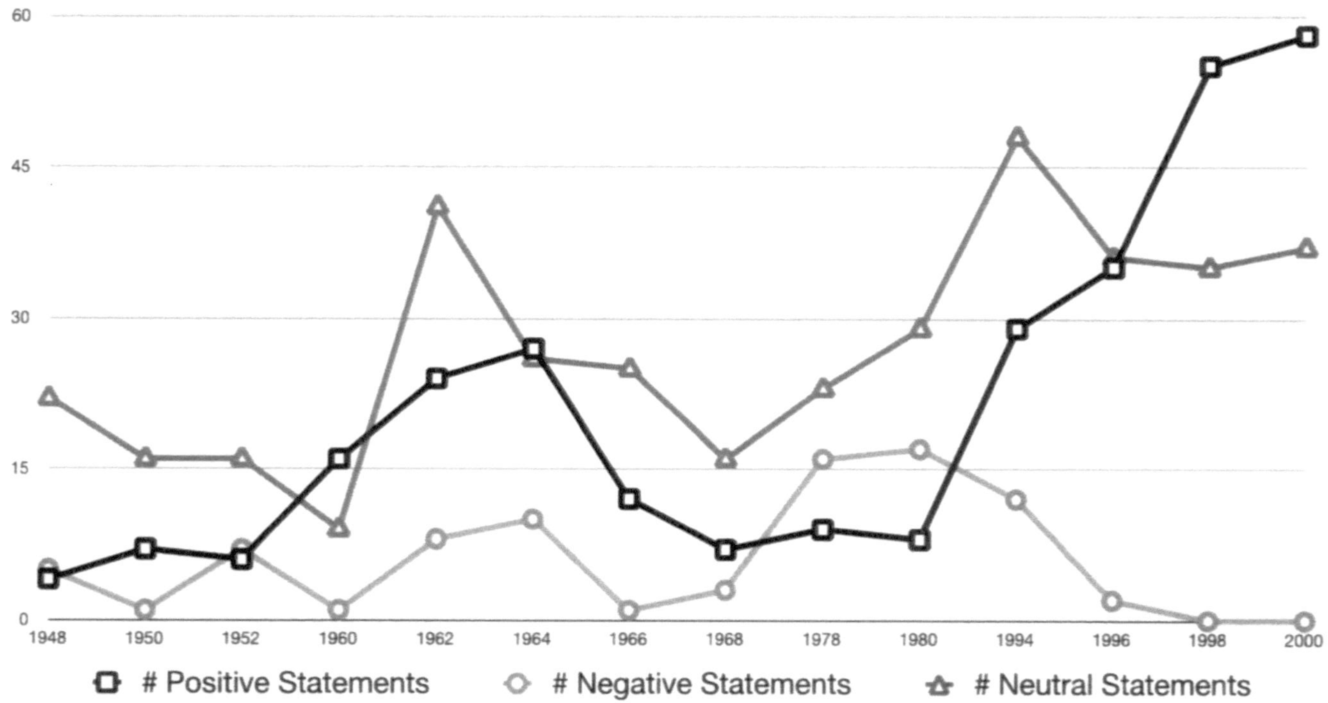

Figure 4.4. Democrat Presidential Economic Statements.
Adapted from *The American Presidency Project*, 2014.

Democratic presidents used 347 negative economic statements, 50 percent of the total statements.

The Public's Perception of the Economy as Predicted by Presidential Rhetoric

I provide multiple models to find the effect of the president's economic rhetoric on the public's perceptions of the economy. Tables 4.2 through 4.5 present the coefficients, odds ratios, and *p*-values as well as the percent changes in odds and the measures of fit. The model, overall, is in line with the hypotheses; the predictor variables, rather than the presidential rhetoric, significantly affect how the public perceives the economy.

The first model (M1) is completely in line with the hypotheses; the party of the president, the respondent, and the extent to which these are the same make a significant difference in the public's perception of the president's handling of the economy. Moreover, the positive rhetoric does not substantively affect whether the overall *public* perceives the economy as good.

In hypothesis 1, when the respondent's attention to politics increases, it makes a significant difference in the public's perception of the president's handling of the economy. As illustrated by table 4.2, the results suggest that the more people pay attention to political information, the more likely they are to perceive the economy as the president portrays it in his positive rhetoric. I think this result should been seen as more of an indicator of social status, those persons who are more economically stable are going to pay more attention to politics. One must use caution while interpreting this result and not assume that *if* people are paying attention to presidential rhetoric about the economy, they are reflecting, in their perceptions, the tone of that economic rhetoric. There is no differentiation between the party of the president and the respondents.

The public is going to interpret what they hear based upon their political predilections, which have been highly influenced by how the political elites they pay attention to have framed the issue (Zaller, 1992). They can only react to what the president is saying based upon what they have learned from the other political elites to whom they pay attention. If the political discourse coming from those political elites differs from what the president is saying, the public will react according to the knowledge that they possess; they will not change their minds and participate in risk in order to stimulate the economy (Eshbaugh-Soha, 2005; Wood, 2007; Wood, Owens, and Durham, 2005; Zaller, 1992). Because the analysis does not include panel-level

Table 4.2. Voter Perception of Their Personal Finances in the Last Year.

	Dependent Variable: Pr (Success = −1 = Worse or 0 = Same or 1 = Better) N = 10,651			
	Predicting Changes in NES Respondent Data			
	Coefficients	*Odds Ratios*	*% Change in Odds*	*p-Values*
Positive Statements	0.1832 (0.2394)	1.201 (0.2876)	20.1	0.444
Respondent Party ID	–0.0442 (0.0092)	0.9568 (0.0088)	– 4.3	0.0000
Presidential Party	0.2083 (0.0756)	1.232 (0.0931)	23.2	0.006
Inflation Rate	0.0798 (0.0186)	1.083 (0.0201)	8.3	0.0000
Unemployment Rate	0.0155 (0.0192)	1.016 (0.0195)	1.6	0.418
Divided Government	0.0872 (0.0891)	1.091 (0.0972)	9.1	0.328
Major Speeches	–0.0121 (0.0168)	0.9880 (0.0166)	– 1.2	0.473
Vote Share	–0.0409 (0.0076)	0.9599 (0.0072)	– 4.0	0.0000
Voted for the Incumbent	0.1325 (0.0594)	1.142 (0.0678)	14.2	0.026
Shared Party ID with President	0.0417 (0.0216)	1.043 (0.0132)	4.3	0.001
Presidential Performance	0.5544 (0.0530)	1.741 (0.0922)	74.1	0.0000
Level of Political Information	0.0833 (0.0184)	1.087 (0.0200)	8.7	0.0000
Presence of a Recession	–0.9049 (0.1169)	0.4046 (0.0473)	–59.5	0.0000
Log Likelihood = – 11,184.88	χ^2 = 931.78 ($p < 0.0000$)			

Adapted from *American National Election Studies*, 2008.

data, the following hypotheses provide a better assessment of the impact of rhetoric on the public's perception.

For hypothesis 2, it is interesting to note, however, that the data indicate it is not significantly more likely that the overall positive economic rhetoric will predict the probability that the overall public will perceive their own personal finances as good despite the current economic conditions. The odds that the public would perceive their personal finances as good over the last year because the president increased the number of positive statements did actually increase. However, the increase was indistinguishable from zero; the result was so insignificant. This result is substantially different from the results Wood (2007) published. By simply using a different data set, there are differences in presidential effectiveness regarding the power of presidential rhetoric. This is interesting given that he states, "[the] debate should now end over whether presidents' words matter [and] future research should turn to other important questions relating to presidential rhetoric and public opinion" (p. 168).

In the second model (M2), using hypothesis 2 again, I found that the data requires a rejection of the null hypothesis. As illustrated by table 4.3, it is significantly more likely that the positive economic rhetoric makes a difference to the public in how they perceive the economy, particularly in the last year. As presented by figure 4.5, the odds of the public perceiving the economy as good in the last year occurring as a result of an increase in the number of positive statements made by the president is the result expected; the more positive statements made by the president, the more likely the respondent thought the economy was worse. These results highly suggest that the president is not able to change the public's perceptions of the economy with positive rhetoric, but show how much they try to change the extant reality.

With regard to the second model, hypotheses 5, 6, and 7, the party of the president, the respondent, and the extent to which these are the same do make a difference in the public's perception of how the president handled the economy in the last year. As in the last model, the closer the party of the respondent and the party of the president get, the more likely the respondent will indicate the president has done a good job with regard to the economy (see table 4.3). As the vote-share that the president received in the previous election increased, the more likely the public's perception of the president's handling of the economy increased. As one might expect, whether or not the respondent voted for the incumbent president made a significant difference in the public's perception of how the president handled the economy (see table 4.3).

The third model (M3) is mostly in-line with the hypotheses. As illustrated by table 4.4, it is significantly more likely that the positive economic rhetoric predicts that the public, across all presidents and respondents, perceive the economy as good in the upcoming year. The odds of the public perceiving the economy as good in the upcoming year, as a result of an increase in the number of positive statements made by the president, were substantial.

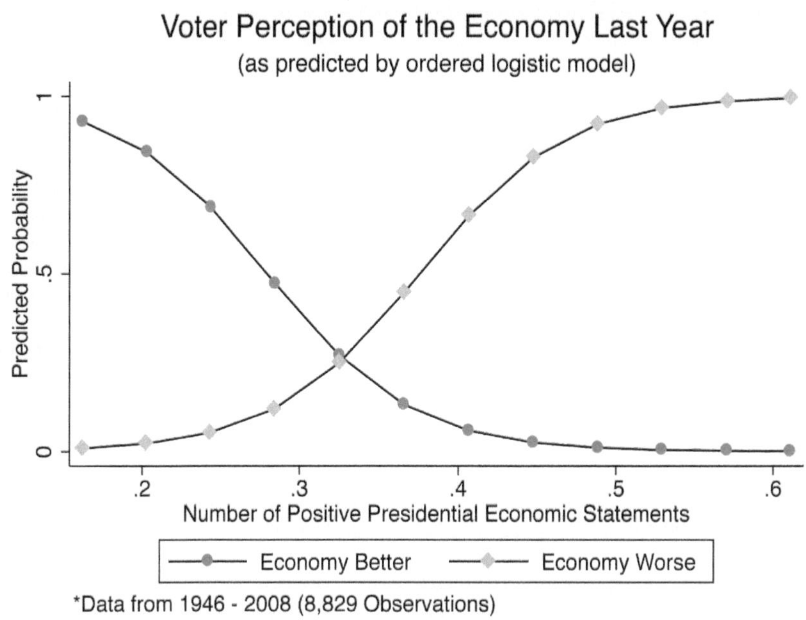

Figure 4.5. Probability of Respondents Perceiving the Economy as Better Last Year. Adapted from *American National Election Studies*, 2008.

When the presidents increased their positive rhetoric, the probability that the public perceived the economy as doing well increased.

The problem with this conclusion, however, is its limitation to definitively state that the optimistic perception of the economy in the upcoming year is a direct result of the positive statements of the president. I think that this result should be viewed quite cautiously for a number of reasons. This analysis was not conducted on individual panel data, which tells us nothing about how the respondents that viewed the upcoming year as positive viewed the economy last year. Such data would tell us specifically if presidents could use their positive rhetoric to change individuals' economic perceptions with positive rhetoric. Secondly, there is an assumption that the respondents have encountered the president's positive rhetoric. As the literature shows, this assumption is unfounded. In addition, this could simply mean that the economic indicators are getting better and that is why the president is talking about the economic expansion more often; the public notices the change in

Table 4.3. Voter Perception of the Economy in the Last Year.

	Dependent Variable: Pr (Success = −1 = Worse or 0 = Same or 1 = Better) N = 8,829			
	Predicting Changes in NES Respondent Data			
	Coefficients	*Odds Ratios*	*% Change in Odds*	*p-Values*
Positive Statements	–21.899 (2.513)	3.09 (7.76)	–100.0	0.0000
Respondent Party ID	–0.0533 (0.0110)	0.9480 (0.0105)	–5.2	0.0000
Presidential Party	–4.713 (0.2697)	0.0089 (0.0024)	–99.1	0.0000
Inflation Rate	–1.409 (0.0971)	0.2445 (0.0237)	–75.1	0.0000
Unemployment Rate	1.277 (0.2016)	0.2790 (0.0562)	–72.1	0.0000
Divided Government	4.203 (0.5109)	66.908 (34.185)	6,590.7	0.0000
Major Speeches	1.233 (0.1107)	3.430 (0.3796)	243.0	0.0000
Vote Share	0.4758 (0.0548)	1.609 (0.0881)	60.9	0.0000
Voted for the Incumbent	0.3741 (0.0548)	1.454 (0.1131)	45.4	0.0000
Shared Party ID with President	0.1077 (0.0162)	1.114 (0.0180)	11.4	0.0000
Presidential Performance	0.9785 (0.0684)	2.660 (0.1817)	X	0.0000
Level of Political Information	0.1393 (0.0238)	1.149 (0.0274)	166.0	0.0000
Log Likelihood – 6,711.3949		$\chi^2 = 5{,}189.25$ ($p < 0.0000$)		

Adapted from *American National Election Studies*, 2008.

the economic indicators rather than trusting the president. Moreover, as a result of the simplicity and limitations of my hypothesis, there could be other conditions besides rhetoric that factor into the public's optimism. Maybe the public is inherently optimistic about the future? Maybe there has been a change in government leadership and this is the impetus for the optimism? There could be any number of factors that play a role. There is no way to measure whether their optimism is a change from a pessimistic outlook about the economy prior to hearing the positive rhetoric from the president. These results simply tell us that, in general, the more positive presidents are about the current economy, the more likely the public reports that it is optimistic about the upcoming economy.

The party of the respondent made a significant difference in the public's perception of the president's handling of the economy in the upcoming year; the more Republican the respondents were, the more likely they thought the economy would be better. I could speculate that it is a result of seven more years that Republicans were in the White House for this analysis. Further, there were more Republican presidents in the time frame of the NES data; Republican respondents view Republican presidents as trusted sources of information wherein they accept what is told to them. As mentioned earlier, those persons with similar economic circumstances typically resonate with the ideas of those presidents that offer messages that impact their own economic predicaments (Brody, 1991).

In this regression, however, the closer the party of the respondent and the party of the president got, it was not more likely that the respondent would indicate the president had done a good job with regard to the economy. Presidential party did not matter in the public's perception either (see table 4.4). These results are noteworthy when compared to the previous analysis. The outcomes suggest that the public pays greater attention to other factors besides the president and their party when contemplating their economic futures.

Across all models (M1, M2, M3), hypotheses 3 and 4 provide a unique contribution to the analysis. As illustrated by table 4.5, the coefficients and odds ratios indicate that party plays a major role in how the public perceives the president's economic leadership. I ran the analyses by presidential party and the party of the respondents: all respondents and all presidents, Republican respondents and Republican presidents, Republican respondents and Democratic presidents, Democratic respondents and Democratic presidents, Independent respondents and Democratic presidents, and Independent respondents and Republican presidents. Differentiating the analysis in this way enabled me to find the effect of the president's positive economic rhetoric on the public's perceptions of the economy in a way that highlights the partisanship of the public and the president.

The differentiated analyses provide mixed results about how the party of the president factors into the perceptions of the respondents and their party affiliation. With regard to Republican respondents, the positive rhetoric from Republican presidents made a highly significant difference in how voters perceived their own personal finances; Republican respondents were 8.97 times more likely to think that their personal finances were better as a result

Table 4.4. Voter Perception of the Economy in the Upcoming Year.

	Dependent Variable: Pr (Success = −1 = Worse or 0 = Same or 1 = Better) N = 10,206			
	Predicting Changes in NES Respondent Data			
	Coefficients	*Odds Ratios*	*% Change in Odds*	*p-Values*
Positive Statements	0.7818 (0.2592)	2.185 (0.5666)	118.5	0.003
Respondent Party ID	−0.0197 (0.0099)	0.9805 (0.0097)	−1.9	0.046
Presidential Party	−0.0653 (0.0817)	0.9366 (0.0765)	−6.3	0.424
Inflation Rate	−0.1050 (0.0197)	0.9004 (0.0178)	−10.0	0.0000
Unemployment Rate	0.0421 (0.0207)	1.043 (0.0215)	4.3	0.042
Divided Government	−0.0952 (0.0932)	0.9092 (0.0847)	−9.1	0.307
Major Speeches	0.0248 (0.0180)	1.025 (0.0185)	2.5	0.169
Vote Share	0.0204 (0.0080)	1.021 (0.0082)	2.1	0.011
Voted for the Incumbent	0.0848 (0.0632)	1.089 (0.0688)	8.8	0.180
Shared Party ID with President	−0.0140 (0.0135)	0.9861 (0.0133)	−1.4	0.301
Presidential Performance	0.4172 (0.0568)	1.518 (0.0862)	51.8	0.0000
Level of Political Information	0.1086 (0.0197)	1.115 (0.0220)	11.5	0.0000
Presence of a Recession	0.4804 (0.1226)	1.617 (0.1982)	61.7	0.0000
Log Likelihood = −9,382.9397	χ^2 = 249.12 (p < 0.0000)			

Adapted from *American National Election Studies*, 2008.

of the positive rhetoric from Republican presidents. Similarly, Democratic respondents were significantly more likely (increased by a factor of 49.26) to think that their personal finances were good as a result of the positive economic rhetoric from Republican presidents. However, despite the positive rhetoric from Republican presidents, the Republican respondents were not more likely to view the economy last year as better or the upcoming economy as better.

Table 4.5. Positive Presidential Statements on the Economy.

	Dependent Variables: Pr (Success = –1 = Worse or 0 = Same or 1 = Better)		
	Predicting Changes in the NES Respondent Data—Differentiated by Political Party		
	Personal Finances	*Economy Last Year*	*Economy Next Year*
	β^/Odds Ratios	*β^/Odds Ratios*	*β^/Odds Ratios*
All Respondents	0.1832 /1.201	–21.90 / 3.09*****	0.7818 / 2.185***
	(0.2394) / (0.2876)	(2.513) / 7.76	(0.2592) / (0.5666)
Rep. Respondents	2.194 / 8.973***	–5.906 / 0.0027*****	–1.559 / 0.2103*
Rep. President	(0.8128) / (7.294)	(0.8910) / 0.0024	(0.8557) / (0.1800)
Rep. Respondents	0.5071 / 1.660	–1.273 / 0.2800*	1.478 / 4.383**
Dem. President	(0.6409) / (1.064)	(0.6727) / (0.1883)	(0.6786) / (2.975)
Dem. Respondents	–0.7579 / 0.4687	–2.592 / 0.0749*****	0.4870 / 1.627
Dem. President	(0.5969) / (0.2797)	(0.6335) / (0.0474)	(0.6201) / (1.009)
Dem. Respondents	3.897 / 49.257*****	–2.801 / 0.0608****	–1.626 / 0.1968**
Rep. President	(0.7287) / (35.893)	(0.8192) / (0.0500)	(0.7759) / (0.1527)
Independent Respondents	1.172 / 3.229	–1.653 / 0.1915**	1.212 / 3.360
Dem. President	(0.8036) / (2.594)	(0.8269) / (0.1584)	(0.8325) / (2.797)
Independent Respondents	2.900 / 18.114***	–2.480 / 0.0838**	–2.503 / 0.0819**
Rep. President	(0.9526) / (17.255)	(0.9948) / (0.0833)	(1.008) / (0.0825)

Adapted from *The American Presidency Project*, 2014.

*$p < 0.1$ **$p < 0.05$ ***$p < 0.01$.

****$p < 0.001$ *****$p < 0.0000$.

The analysis does not produce the same type of results for Republican respondents and Democratic presidents or Democratic respondents and Democratic presidents. However, Republican respondents were significantly more likely (increased by a factor of 4.38) to think that the economy was going to be good in the next year as a result of the positive economic rhetoric from the Democratic presidents. Democratic respondents were significantly less likely to think that the economy will be better next year as a result of the positive economic rhetoric from Republican presidents.[9]

Conclusion

This analysis sought to expand upon many arguments in presidential economic rhetoric literature, namely, that the president can use positive, optimistic rhetoric to shape how the public perceives their economic conditions (Eshbaugh-Soha, 2006; Wood, 2007; 2012; Wood, Owens, and Durham, 2005). More specifically, this analysis provided two specific components. The first showed the extent and the manner in which the presidents pay attention to indicators of the economy's strength or weakness. Secondly, it assessed how the public perceives the economy as presented by the president.

This chapter attempted to answer whether the president could use his positive, optimistic rhetoric to make the public think that he is a strong economic leader who was taking the country in the right economic direction, which would, in turn, motivate the public to take economic risks in spending, investing, and loaning—making the economy better. The results in this chapter, however, suggest that the president is not overly successful when using positive or negative economic rhetoric to change how his economic leadership is perceived by the public.

By utilizing the NES data, it seems one cannot simply make grandiose claims about the persuasive power of the tone (positive/negative) or optimistic outlook of the presidential rhetoric and its effectiveness in shaping economic behavior or establishing a perception of leadership. The justification for using one data indicator to correlate or predict the outcomes of presidential rhetoric does not withstand scrutiny. Therefore, this chapter offered a more comprehensive framework for approaching this analysis. A more comprehensive assessment of presidential rhetoric suggests that there is a lack of connection and influence with the public, particularly there appears to be a disconnect between how presidents have discussed the economy and how the public perceives the economy (Wood, 2007; Wood, Owens, and Durham, 2005).

The extant research does not take into consideration how consumers process political discourse, the extent to which they pay attention to political issues, and their reactions to political rhetoric. Therefore, the literature has not addressed, comprehensively, the limitations present in the public's reactions and responses to presidential economic rhetoric; it has not fully considered that the "consumer" is going to view the economy differently from what is actually transpiring in economic indicators. This creates a challenge for presidents to motivate the public to perceive the economy as good. In other words, because the economic indicators are changing positively, does not necessarily translate to the consumer viewing the economy as better due to something that the president has done.

The president's relationship with the public is constrained by the limitations of audience, political predilections, and political party values. The economic rhetoric from the president is unable to definitively influence or shape the public's perceptions regarding the economy as some of the literature suggests. My research suggests that the way the public perceives economic conditions cannot fully be determined by the tone of presidential economic rhetoric; the rhetoric is not able to predict, with statistical significance, the probability that the public will perceive a good economy as a result of positive presidential rhetoric. Party identification makes more of a difference in how the public views the economy than the tone of presidential rhetoric. The predispositions persons have about which party is better able to offer them economic security in the future most likely determines for which president (Republican or Democrat) that person will support (Lockerbie, 2008). These data reinforce the notion that the public receives its information from party elites and approves or disapproves of it based upon the "elite" providing the message, complicating the president's ability to lead the public economically (DiClerico, 1993; Wolf and Holian, 2006).

Presidents have increased their rhetoric regarding the economy. However, the increase has not brought them success in shaping the economy. The public's perceptions regarding the economy do not reflect the tone of presidential rhetoric, despite many instances of positive economic speeches; there is a higher probability that the public perceives their economic situation from other externalities, such as respondent party affiliation and economic conditions, rather than from the tone of the president's economic rhetoric. It is clear from multiple models and significance tests that the individuals do not, overall, think about the economy in the way that the presidents would like—whether it is their current economic situation, their perception of the future economy, or their own personal finances. The president's messages are not getting to the public from the president in the way that presidents want. The changed media, the disconnected and truly uninformed public, and the negativity, all contribute to the president's diminished capacity to lead the public. Regardless of presidential attempts to tailor their rhetoric to meet specific needs, they are incredibly unsuccessful, in nearly every way; the public does not change their perceptions about the economy when the president tries to convince them (Cohen, 2008; Edwards, 2003; Eshbaugh-Soha and Peake, 2006; 2011).

Notes

1. Wood, Owens, and Durham (2005) maintain that dividing the average quarterly U.S. personal consumption expenditures by national income provides this description.
2. The argument maintains that the high consumer confidence levels are directly correlated with the positive rhetoric from the president and are evidence of the direct affect the presidents have upon the economy. There is a concern with using only these data and making grandiose claims about the definitiveness of presidential rhetoric's effect; there is no empirical connection suggesting that politics or presidential rhetoric influences this index. There is literature that shows a correlation between the Index and its effect/influence on political decision-making, but that is a completely different argument (Eshbaugh-Soha, 2005; Wood, 2007).
3. The NES data (1948–2008) source covers more of the rhetorical presidency (1913–2013) than the Consumer Confidence Index (1967–2011).
4. It is reasonable to assume that those participating in the NES have, at the very least, a political connection between their ideas of the economy and those of the president, given the context of the survey and the specific questions asked about the president and the economy. One can easily infer that the context of a survey dealing with politics and the public forces the participant to cognitively associate the economy and the president.
5. President Obama's national healthcare policy speech is the paradigmatic example, wherein he was only able to garner about 35 percent of viewers.
6. I selected these administrations because they are representative of the rhetorical presidency. Moreover, the data from the NES website is available during those dates.
7. The NES survey uses a multivariable survey that has a Likert-type scale to determine responses about people's opinions on political issues.
8. www.electionstudies.org/studypages/download/datacenter_all.htm.
9. The analysis also shows that Independent respondents were less likely to believe Democratic presidents than they were to believe Republican presidents about the prospects of the future economy and the past economy. The exception, however, consists of Independent respondents thinking that the economy next year will be worse by a factor of 0.082 as a result of the positive economic rhetoric of the Republican presidents (see table 4.5).

CHAPTER FIVE

Congressional Actions as Preeminent Economic Leadership

It is the duty of the President to propose and it is the privilege of the Congress to dispose.

—Franklin D. Roosevelt (Woolley and Peters, 2014 —"Franklin D. Roosevelt, 1937")

President Clinton and the 1993 Budget Struggle

Presidents try to influence the Congress by "going public" with the direction they want for economic policy, whether it is nationally or locally (Canes-Wrone, 2001; Cohen, 2010; Edwards, 1995; Kernell, 2007).[1] They use rhetorical cues and signals to the Congress that address the economic changes they want and what they are willing to do to get Congress to address the economic conditions (Edwards, 2003; Eshbaugh-Soha, 2005).[2] The problem, however, is that Congress creates its own mechanisms of policy information distribution that enable individual members, who are less informed, to garner policy expertise, thus, bypassing the president's signals—whether those signals are rhetorical or mechanisms of informal power such as approval ratings and party control of Congress (Krehbiel, 1991). This suggests that Congress is not passively waiting for the president to provide leadership on economic policy, nor are they overly receptive to his persuasive attempts. Members of Congress are concerned with making their own versions of good policy and their own reelection, which may take them in a different direction than where the president is trying to lead (Fenno, 1978; Jacobs and Shapiro, 2000; Mayhew, 1989).

Not long after President Clinton assumed the presidency, he proposed an economic policy plan and budget that was politically ambitious and highly controversial. The budget signaled a shift in priorities and economic policy. Prior to his proposition, however, Clinton was faced with reneging on a campaign promise wherein he vowed to give the middle-class a tax cut (Pfiffner, 2001). Given the rapidly increasing deficit and discussions of how that deficit would impact future fiscal policy and the financial viability of the United States, after serious debate and consideration, President Clinton proposed an energy tax and a tax increase on the affluent citizens. According to projections, the changes, if enacted, would have eliminated the federal deficit by $500 billion in five years. President Clinton said

> And it [budget proposal] has a deficit reduction program that will increase the savings available for the private sector to invest, will lower interest rates, will decrease the percentage of the Federal budget claimed by interest payments, and decrease the risk of financial market disruptions that could adversely affect our economy.
>
> Over the long run, all this will bring us a higher rate of economic growth, improved productivity, more high-quality jobs, and an improved economic competitive position in the world. In order to accomplish both increased investment and deficit reduction, something no American government has ever been called upon to do at the same time before, spending must be cut and taxes must be raised. (Woolley and Peters, 2014—"William J. Clinton, February 17, 1993")

The Republican Party opposition to the proposal was severe and long-standing; it existed in each step of the process. The resistance and the acceptance of the new direction in economic policy reached complete partisanship. The votes in the House of Representatives (243–183) and in the Senate (54–45) were cast strictly along party lines. Not a single Republican member of Congress, senators or representatives, supported President Clinton's economic platform for reform. Moreover, there were a few Democrats that opposed the plan as well. President Clinton said

> We have been working for days to get this done. And finally, yesterday afternoon they gave up. So I called the folks that had given up, and I said, go back to the table. We've got to have some discipline in this budget, so that if we tell people we're going to make the cuts, we do it . . . a lot of the Republicans who might otherwise want to vote with us got into a position where they said they wouldn't vote for any tax. (Woolley and Peters, 2014—"William J. Clinton, May 27, 1993")

The budget resolution, actually, was one of the easier steps for the Clinton administration's new program. In fact, during the negations for the reconciliation bill the tension and opposition became more intense. A most difficult battle ensued in the House of Representatives, requiring constant attention from President Clinton (Pfiffner, 2001). He won the vote (219–213); yet, the support had dwindled significantly—thirty-eight Democrats voted against the reconciliation bill. In the Senate, the fight was just as contentious. The energy tax was dropped and replaced with a gas tax. Again, Clinton won the vote (49–49) when Vice President Al Gore voted to break the tie. Despite the success and difficulty, the issue was not over completely. The differences in the reconciliation bills had to be fixed. The process was more of the same. The votes were nearly identical; Clinton lost one more Democrat vote in the House (Pfiffner, 2001). President Clinton said, after the vote,

> After twelve long years, we can say to the American people tonight we have laid the foundation for the renewal of the American dream. The days of endless gridlock, rising deficits, and trickle-down economics are over. The days of economic growth and real opportunity for the working families of this country have begun. (Woolley and Peters, 2014—"William J. Clinton, August 6, 1993")

President Clinton only garnered 43 percent of the popular vote in the 1992 election, giving him just a plurality, but not a majority. He did win a heavy number of the electoral votes (370), however. In addition, he won thirty-two states and Washington, DC, compared to George H. W. Bush's eighteen states. Given the electoral advantage with which Clinton won, it is no surprise that he entered the presidency with a 58 percent approval rating—hovering near that percentage until soon after the House of Representatives first voted to approve the budget resolution (Woolley and Peters, 2014). As the weeks ensued and more discussions of the shift in economic policy engendered further battles and controversies of political will, President Clinton's approval ratings steadily decreased through August 1993, wherein it was as low as 36 percent before plateauing around the midforties during the final votes for the legislation (Woolley and Peters, 2014). It seems, however, that President Clinton's approval ratings were not at a high enough level to garner a mandate for economic policy change, although they steadily increased after the vote.

The timing of this shift in economic policy and deficit reduction facilitated in its success, as did President Clinton's approval ratings and majority in the Congress. President Clinton introduced this bill during the first one hundred days in office, his "honeymoon" period (Barrett and Eshbaugh-Soha, 2007). Presidents tend to obtain more legislative victories during this period of their administration (Light, 1999). It is no surprise that President Clinton was able to advance this economic plan through the legislature at the time he did, facing the externalities that existed (Eshbaugh-Soha, 2010). The Congress had fifty-seven Democratic senators and 258 Democratic members in House of Representatives. Moreover, budget resolutions do not face the threat of the filibuster in the Senate, requiring only a majority vote. However, the difficulties that President Clinton encountered while attempting to build a legislative coalition highlight the fundamental argument of this chapter, namely, that presidents struggle to influence Congress and are typically successful in a specific context.

Presidents have increasingly endeavored to influence Congress, whether or not the influence is substantial in economic policy is debatable. It is, however, difficult for presidential rhetoric to shape the economic behavior of Congress, because their ability to do so is too constrained by the externalities and the powers Congress possesses. Congress has goals that may be different from or even contrary to those of the president (Light, 1999). The Congress and possibly each of its members may have more important goals to which their constituents want them to attend. In fact, some members, particularly those of the opposing party, may have a primary goal of obstructing the president's objectives for the economy. Moreover, the major political parties are a weakened institution; the tension has increased to the point where "bipartisanship" is a liability for political actors. This makes it difficult for presidents to build coalitions, which are necessary to accomplish any passage of legislation.

The following chapter offers a quantitative explanation about the extent to which presidents are influential with Congress, one of the most significant economic actors. How can the president assert influence over one incredibly important economic actor if he is competing with their active agendas, constituent demands, timing, and partisanship? The findings serve to highlight the glaring flaw in the prevailing argument that presidential rhetoric matters in the sense that it can persuade or influence—as the most important economic actors often need to oppose the president's economic plans to remain legitimate in the eyes of their own constituents. The findings provide a contribution to the discussion in the literature on presidential economic relations with the Congress, particularly their capacity to shape economic policy (Barrett, 2004; 2005; Barrett and Eshbaugh-Soha, 2007; Bond and Fleisher, 2000a; Canes-Wrone, 2001; Canes-Wrone and de Marchi, 2002; Eshbaugh-Soha, 2005; Pfiffner, 2001; Light, 1999).

Nevertheless, I consider the literature regarding Congress and the economy and address how presidential rhetoric factors into their economic behavior. The chapter then moves to determining the external considerations to which Congress pays attention more than presidential rhetoric: time, approval ratings, and public expectations. From ascertaining the overall ineffectiveness of presidents "going public" and the limitations they face in building coalitions, I posit a theory and empirical model that suggests Congress is more responsive to current economic conditions and their own reelection prospects (via their constituency demands) when considering economic policy directions and decisions.

Congress and the Economy

The influence Congress has over the economy is substantial; it is a creator of fiscal policy and also affects monetary policy[3] (Kiewiet and McCubbins, 1985; Kiewiet, 1983). According to Wildavsky and Caiden (2003), the congressional budget process has changed substantially in recent decades. The Congressional Budget Act of 1974 established the top-down budget process, which created an exhaustive budget resolution. This was created by a new budget committee in each House, and supported by the new Congressional Budget Office. According to Niskanen (1971), the Balanced Budget and Emergency Deficit Control Act of 1985 created the statutory deficit reduction schedule and procedures for implementation. In 1990, the Congress passed the Budget Enforcement Act, which categorized budgeting: defense, nondefense discretionary, and entitlements (Dolan, Frendreis, and Tatalovich, 2008). Wildavsky and Caiden (2003) argue that the new process comes from a fundamental change in thought about the role of the federal government and intergovernmental relationships, namely, a disagreement about which institution should be in charge of fiscal policy. These changes create tension and a struggle for power between the Congress and the president.

In fact, congressional action on the economy can transform the president's economic agenda (Leuchtenburg, 1995). For instance, Congress wants to assert more authority over the budget. Creating the Impoundment Control Act of 1974, which restricts the president's power to curb spending for any reason exemplifies this masterfully. Congress has the power and authority, through the budget and the budgetary process, to create changes and transform many economic indicators with which the president is concerned, particularly with expenditures wherein they assert their dominance (Pack, 1988).

The president understands this reality and often seeks to mitigate intrusion of Congress and how they influence the direction of economic policy. To shape economic policy, the president must persuade or bargain with Congress, which is essential to building coalitions that will offer opportunities for policy development (Neustadt, 1991). Therefore, the president needs to have congressional support; his persuasive task is to convince Congress that what the administration wants to do economically is what Congress ought to do as a whole and for each individual member's constituents.

The President and Congress

Understanding that presidential power is externally controlled is crucial to determining the president's relationships with Congress and the economy (Light, 1999). There are many elements to consider when deciphering how limited the presidents are in using rhetoric to shape the external pressures influencing their decision-making. First, Congress has goals that may be different or even contrary to those of the president; there is congressional competition for agenda space. Congress, and possibly each of its members, may have more important matters to which their constituents want them to attend. In fact, some members, particularly those of the opposing party, may have a primary goal of obstructing the president's goals for the economy.

Secondly, the policy process is more fragmented; there are more steps in the law-making process with the increase of subsystem politics. As illustrated by figure 5.1, the political conflicts make producing economic legislation more difficult. Presidential influence in Congress has rapidly declined, particularly with regard to their standing with the political parties (Light, 1999). The parties are a weakened institution now that divided government is such a common occurrence (Bond and Fleisher, 2000b). The conflict has increased to the point where bipartisanship is a liability for political actors. Building coalitions has become an obstreperous endeavor for presidents. Without the coalitions, legislative accomplishment is nearly impossible. Presidents are simply not as influential, legislatively, as they once were.

Thirdly, Congress has a vast agenda with which the president must compete; it is more likely to ignore requests from the presidents, despite rhetorical cues and signals (Edwards and Barrett, 2000; Edwards and Wood, 1999; Light, 1999). Congress has limits as to what it can even consider because of the time constraints of the legislative session, the institutional and constituency-responsibilities, and the amount of externalities with which it must contend. Moreover, each request has a number of steps it must pass

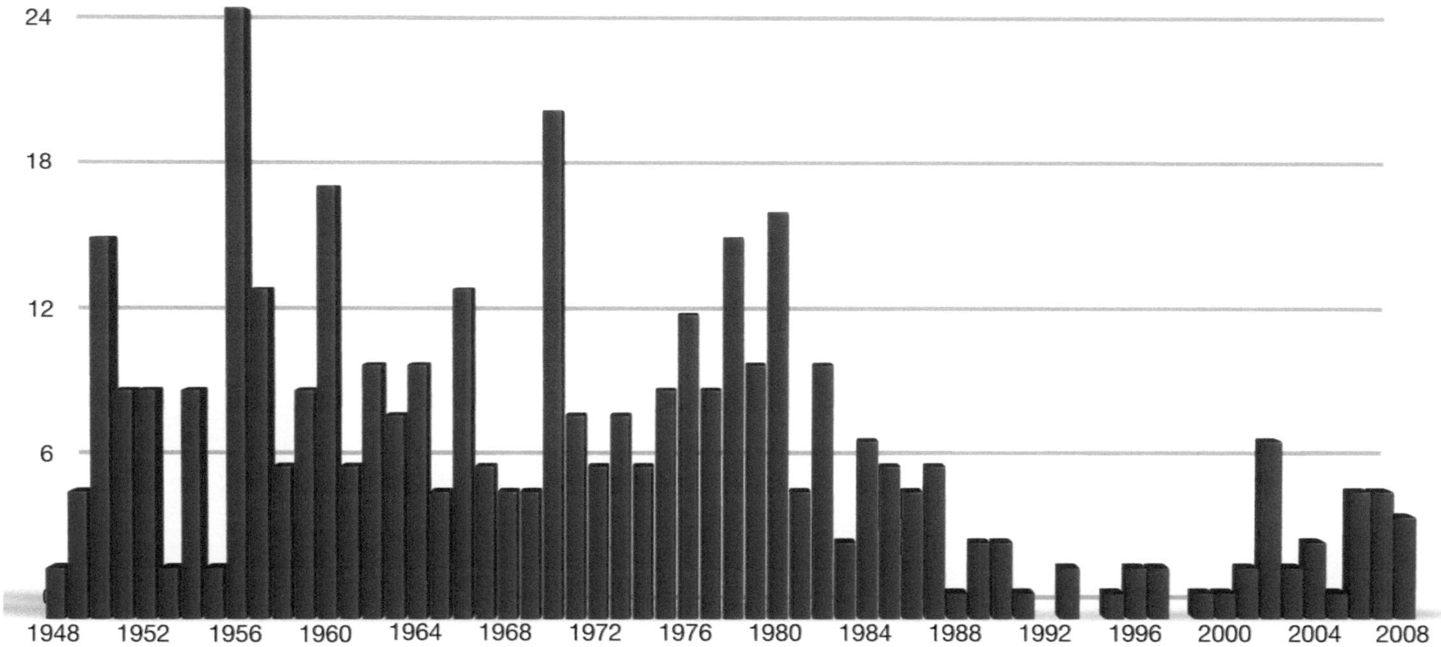

Figure 5.1. Economic Public Laws each Congressional Year.
Adapted from *Policy Agendas Project*, 2014.

through, committees and hearings, before it can receive full consideration (Cox and McCubbins, 2007; Krehbiel, 1991). Presidents have to limit their requests from Congress to coincide with the goals of Congress in order to strategically maximize their legislative accomplishments (Light, 1999). Therefore, often their priorities are nearly forgotten in the agenda of Congress (Edwards and Wood, 1999; Light, 1999).

Going Public as a Bargaining Mechanism

Presidents take their issues public and try to mobilize their constituencies; reaching out to the public is a way to increase their legislative influence, they think (Eshbaugh-Soha and Peake, 2005). Presidents go public because of declining party mechanisms; it is difficult for them to form coalitions with Congress. Presidents may have been able to use their party, in years past, as a bargaining tool, but party dynamics have changed substantially. The practice of going public is in direct contradiction, however, to the notion of persuading or bargaining; it eradicates the "kinds of exchanges . . . for the American political system to function properly" (Kernell, 2007, p. 3). This approach leaves no room for compromise; it keeps Congress from receiving the credit and the benefits from doing what was required. Moreover, it imposes all negative political costs on those who do not do what the president requests (Kernell, 2007). This creates direct opposition to the president's requests and engenders a contentious environment wherein the president gets less than he wants legislatively (Canes-Wrone, 2001; Kernell, 2007).

Presidents have recently recognized that this strategy is not effective, particularly the national element (Cohen, 2010; Kernell, 2007). To accommodate, presidents have started "going local" to garner support for their policies (Cohen, 2010). Presidents capitalize on their high approval ratings in the party-friendly local districts they visit. The idea is that the local newspapers will portray them and their message in a more positive narrative, which will shape the perspectives of their constituencies. The positive narrative, however, does not translate to more policy victories (Cohen, 2010). In recent years, presidents have not gone public as often as one might expect (Barrett, 2005). They tend to do so only for existing legislative proposals that they support and for those that have a chance of getting through both houses of Congress (Barrett, 2004). Leading Congress through positive rhetoric is not a viable option for the presidents (Eshbaugh-Soha and Peake, 2006).

The Importance of Coalition Building in the Congress

Congress often purposefully restricts the president's legislative policy development abilities (DiClerico, 2000). The interaction with Congress is one of the most complicated relationships that presidents have to maintain. They must convince both houses of Congress to support their economic programs (Eshbaugh-Soha and Peake, 2005). To further complicate the relationship, the committee system of Congress has the potential to seriously impede the president. Without favorable committee chairpersons, their legislation could potentially remain in committee indefinitely (DiClerico, 2000). And, if it does leave the committee, it still has to overcome the filibuster threat. The presidents need party loyalists in order to build coalitions that will support their economic policies. Building coalitions is the only effective way to accomplish anything legislatively (Arnold, 1990; Barrett and Eshbaugh-Soha, 2007; Canes-Wrone, 2006; Edwards, 1980; Jones, 1994; Neustadt, 1991). Despite the relationship that exists, the president needs to work with the Congress because of its vital role in the economy (Eshbaugh-Soha and Peake, 2005).

Party affiliation is a strong predictor of presidential success in the legislature; as unified government increases, the presidents are more successful legislatively (Bond and Fleisher, 2000). Divided government engenders problems for the legislative process. Even though Mayhew (1989) argues that there is really no difference in the amount of legislation produced under divided government, there is an argument to be made that the substance of the legislation is different or even compromised during divided government (Barrett and Eshbaugh-Soha, 2007; Kernell, 2007). Unified government provides the president with more opportunity to gain legislation that advances his agenda (Barrett and Eshbaugh-Soha, 2007; Conley, 2002). Presidents can be more effective legislatively during unified government when they make their preferences known (Conley, 2002).

Presidents have, recently, had a difficult time motivating their own party to support their policies, however (Bond and Fleisher, 2000b). The declining party mechanisms are the reason the president cannot form coalitions with Congress (Brace and Hinckley, 1992). Party politics has become more contentious and presents a challenge to the president (Bond and Fleisher, 2000b). Party cohesion, based upon ideology, is not an element upon which the presidents can fully depend (Bond and Fleisher, 1990).

The problem is that *party* is no longer the "gold standard of presidential influence"; even though presidents still need their party to do anything; it is no guarantee that the party will help (Light, 1999, p. 12). The strength of parties varies over time, which limits the president's ability to use them to his advantage (Jacobson, 2000). This is especially true given that presidential strength varies over their time in office. The presence or absence of divided government or unified government can significantly influence economic legislative outcomes (Canes-Wrone, 2006). This is even more pronounced when the president and Congress are dealing with the budget or specific appropriations bills (Brady and Volden, 2006; Krehbiel, 1998).

The president cannot rely on parties to further his agenda (Krehbiel, 1998). In fact, what matters are the preferences of individual members of Congress, particularly the median member. In other words, policies and bills cannot even go to the president until they pass the majority in the House and the filibuster threat in the Senate (Brady and Volden, 2006). In other words, individuals, in a particular context, are able to derail what presidents want; it is not the parties (Krehbiel, 1998). The president needs to contend with the goals of each member. Granted, there are going to be times when the goals and preferences of the president are the same with many of those in Congress, typically by party ideology. Nonetheless, one must still consider the importance of the party, particularly because majority parties have more resources at their disposal in Congress to arrange committees and the agenda, which will in turn affect the president's goals and agenda (Aldrich and Rohde, 2000).

Approval Ratings and Congressional Response

Presidents seek to make their approval ratings as high as possible because it will provide them with the opportunity to secure more policy success in Congress (Canes-Wrone and de Marchi, 2002). The research, however, has provided mixed results as to the ability of approval ratings to make presidents more successful legislatively. Canes-Wrone and de Marchi (2002) postulate that higher approval ratings will only make presidents more legislatively successful if there is a combination of salience and complexity or lack of understanding concerning the policy implications. Even for this to work, the president must posses an approval rating that exceeds 50 percent. More typically, when member constituents are informed about an important policy, Congress will ignore presidential requests in favor of those of their constituents (Rivers and Rose, 1985).

There is an inevitable decline in presidential approval ratings that cannot be overcome (Brace and Hinckley, 1992). A coalition of minorities get upset and decrease their support. The second term of any president is more difficult for presidential success legislatively and their approval ratings decline much more quickly. The higher their public approval ratings are, the more they get done in Congress. Also, success in the Congress means they get higher approval ratings. It is a cyclical process.

The success of presidential requests for legislation depends upon their approval rating when they make the request (Kernell, 2007). Presidents anticipate that a citizen is more likely to support their policy requests and petition Congress about it if their approval rating is high, indicating previous success and effectiveness. Thus, Congress is responsive to its own electorate and how they view the president's popularity (Edwards, 1980). For instance, congressional members pay particular attention to the president's approval ratings within subgroups such as party favorability. Congressional success based upon presidential popularity is not consistent over time.

The Effect of *Time* on Presidential Relations with Congress

Timing influences the success of legislative accomplishment (Barrett and Eshbaugh-Soha, 2007). Presidents tend to obtain more legislative victories during the honeymoon period of their administration (Neustadt, 1991). This honeymoon period begins with the election of their first term in office and typically continues throughout the first one hundred days (Eshbaugh-Soha, 2005; Light, 1999). Presidents are at the height of their approval during this time, typically; they should be able to advance their agenda and succeed legislatively more significantly than at any other time (Eshbaugh-Soha, 2010). As their time in office continues, their ability to successfully bargain with or influence Congress depreciates (Barrett and Eshbaugh-Soha, 2007; Light, 1999).

Presidential influence and resources begin to decline immediately upon assuming the presidency. Light (1999) argues that presidents suffer from "the cycle of decreasing influence" (p. 39). In other words, as they continue onward in their presidency, they lose influence and bargaining power with those in Congress. The president has to select policy actions early as possible, because he is only effective with Congress in the first months of his presidency. Therefore, the president has to push for Congressional actions on the economy early in order to be successful. Presidents, typically, have 1,460 days in office. In order to get a better understanding of how their time is spent, subtract 365 days for the reelection campaign, 183 days for midterm elections, 183 days to get his administration up and running, another 183 days to end the administration, and about sixty days for vacations (Light, 1999). Therefore, presidents have about 486 days to do their jobs; that is less than two years. Furthermore, if presidents are reelected to a second term, time moves faster than in the first term. In fact, the president is considered a "lame duck by the end of the second year" (p. 17). Light (1999) provides a quote from Harry McPherson, an aid to President Johnson, which is paradigmatic of the difficulty and importance of time for the presidents; it is worth repeating. Johnson supposedly said the following to his staff after becoming president:

> You've got to give it all you can that first year. Doesn't matter what kind of majority you come in with. You've got just one year when they treat you right and before they start worrying about themselves. The third year, you lose votes. . . . The fourth year's all politics. You can't put anything through when half of the Congress is thinking about how to beat you. So you've got one year (McPherson, 1972, p. 268, quoted in Light, 1999, p. 13).

Economic Expectations and Conditions

The public typically has specific expectations for most economic conditions (Dolan, Frendreis, and Tatalovich, 2008). Despite events of national importance, the public regards the economy, specifically, unemployment and inflation, as the number one issue on their minds. Economic conditions are substantively linked to the public's decision-making regarding governmental actors. Such economic externalities often influence governmental decision-making. It has something to do with the public expectations and how they have been growing (Brace and Hinckley, 1992). Mainly because politicians have been promising more, even overpromising in order to resonate with the public in hopes and anticipation of reelection, higher approval numbers, or historical legacy.

Congress often considers these economic conditions when acting politically, particularly macroeconomic indicators such as unemployment and inflation. Moreover, when the U.S. economy is in a recession, constituency demands often necessitate a response legislatively (Dolan, Frendreis, and Tatalovich, 2008). The rate of unemployment often clouds the perceptions the public has of elected officials (Zaller, 1998). When the economy is doing well, Americans have a higher approval of government. The opposite is also true; when the economy is doing poorly, Americans disapprove of government (Edwards and Wayne, 1985; Wood, 2004). High unemployment can cause members to lose reelection and high inflation rates can do the same. The legislative response helps Congress redirect the attention from the economic indicator to more salient issues that Congress is handling well (Lowry and Shipan, 2002).

Given Congress's institutional mandates for economic considerations, as well as the public's expectations, they must factor the economy into their agenda (Hoffman and Howard, 2010). Congress's relationship with the economy and their constituents casts some doubt on the claim that the president, through his rhetorical actions, is able to garner congressional responses regarding economic effects or indicators (Eshbaugh-Soha and Peake, 2005; Rockman, 1984). It is more likely that Congress would pay attention to economic indicators rather than presidential rhetoric when considering economic actions.

Hypotheses for Predicting Changes in Congressional Behavior

The president's economic agenda (fiscal and monetary policy) faces external limitations from Congress; it is important to ascertain if aggregated economic rhetoric can create an impetus for action from this economic actor or if their rhetoric is too constrained by the externalities of Congress and the powers it possesses. The results from these hypotheses provides two specific components that show when a president pays attention to indicators of the economy's strength or weakness and the extent to which the Congress pays attention to what he is saying and if that rhetoric shapes how Congress reacts to it.

H1: Negative economic rhetoric will not prompt congressional hearings on the economy and will not prompt congressional action regarding economic legislation.

H2: Positive economic rhetoric will not prompt congressional hearings on the economy and will not prompt congressional action regarding economic legislation.

H3: The number of presidential requests for legislation will not prompt congressional hearings on the economy and will not prompt congressional action regarding economic legislation.

H4: Higher presidential approval ratings will not prompt congressional hearings on the economy and will not prompt congressional action regarding economic legislation.

H5: The declining party mechanisms have diluted the effects of unified government and lessened the president's ability to utilize it to shape congressional economic behavior.

H6: The petitions for economic actions in the first one hundred days in office from the president should predict more congressional hearings on the economy and more economic legislation.

H7: The presidents should be able to convince Congress to act on the economy in the first years of their administration. Presidents who are considered a "lame duck" are not able to effectively convince Congress to act on the economy.

H8: The unemployment rate will prompt congressional hearings on the economy and will prompt congressional action regarding economic legislation.

H9: The inflation rate will prompt congressional hearings on the economy and will prompt congressional action regarding economic legislation.

H10: The presence of a recession will prompt congressional hearings on the economy and will prompt congressional action regarding economic legislation.

Empirical Design

Using the data from the *Policy Agendas Project* and *The American Presidency Project*, from presidents Harry S. Truman through George W. Bush—1948 through 2008, I estimated the relationship between presidential economic rhetoric and congressional behavior. Connecting these two data sources offers a unique look into the president's ability to shape the economic behavior of Congress. As illustrated by figure 5.2, I tracked presidential speeches, cues, and signals that dealt with the economy and aggregated the rhetoric monthly to match the *Policy Agendas Project* data. This exercise enabled me to ascertain the effectiveness of presidential economic rhetoric and the congressional response. I was then able to determine if economic rhetoric could predict congressional actions regarding the economy. In line with the aforementioned hypotheses, the analysis needed two separate models (M1 = presidential rhetoric's ability to predict congressional hearings on the economy—as a measure of attention to the economy, M2 = presidential rhetoric's ability to predict economic legislation).

Statistical Method

The analysis required a *count data regression analysis* (negative binomial) to determine the effect of the presidential attention on congressional attention. I modeled the number of congressional hearings on the economy (M1) and public laws (M2) from Congress as a result of presidential economic rhetoric. The negative binomial regression model allowed me to have a *Vuong test*. Such a statistical method showed me the best methodology to use for measuring the effect of aggregated economic rhetoric on the likelihood that Congress would respond to the cues, signals, and threats in the president's rhetoric. The model's dispersion parameter "alpha" is significantly different from zero. The data were overdispersed, which means that using a negative

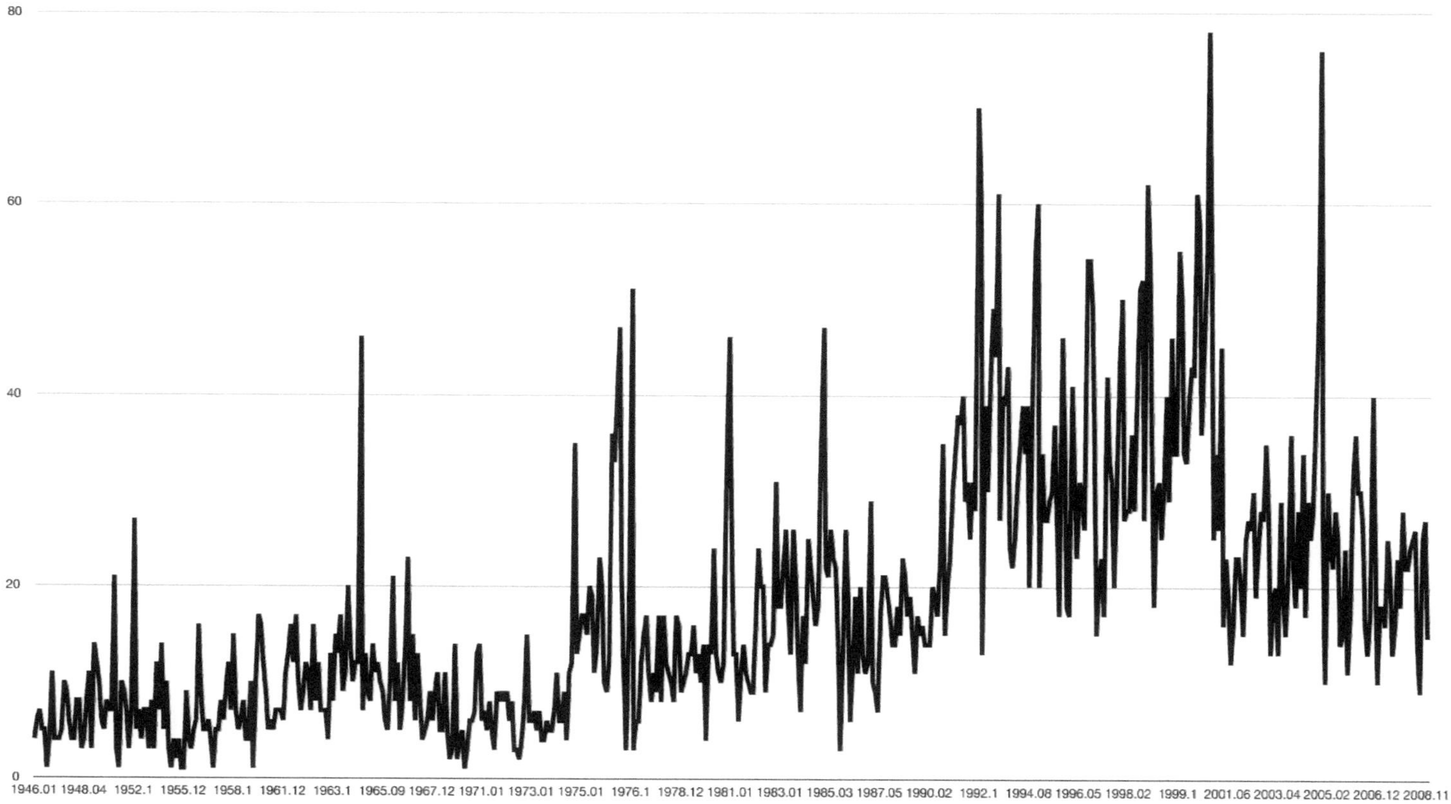

Figure 5.2. Monthly Presidential Speeches (1946–2008).
Adapted from *The American Presidency Project*, 2014.

binomial model provided better results than using a regular *Poisson* model. The regression provides the predicted probabilities of a one-unit change in the presence of the dependent variables, *congressional hearings* and *public laws*, in this analysis of 610 and 369 units of analysis, respectively. The log likelihood chi-squared values for the *congressional hearings* variable (196.51) and the *public laws* variable (53.29) were all significant at the 0.0000 alpha level (see tables 5.2 and 5.3). The regression took the form,

PR ($CB_{i,t}$ = 0 or # Hearings) = $\alpha + \gamma$ *Presidential Rhetoric*$_{i,t}$ + γ *Presidential Influence*$_{i,t}$ + γ *Economic Indicators*$_{i,t}$ + $\hat{\beta_1}$ *Divided Government*$_{i,t}$ + $\hat{e}_{i,t}$ (M1 and M2)

This regression tested whether Congress responds to presidential rhetoric or externalities. The specification controls for the $CB_{i,t}$, wherein the *i* represents the aggregated number of congressional hearings and public laws as counted from the *Policy Agendas Project* or the aggregated number of each vector in each period *t* (monthly from 1948 through 2008). Therefore, I regressed the $CB_{i,t}$ on the rhetoric of the presidents—a vector of various expressions of their rhetoric ($\hat{\beta_1}$ *Number of Positive Economic Statements*$_{i,t}$ + $\hat{\beta_2}$ *Number of Negative Economic Statements*$_{i,t}$ + $\hat{\beta_3}$ *Number of Statements Made in the 1st 100 Days of an Administration*$_{i,t}$ + $\hat{\beta_4}$ *Number of Requests for Economic Legislation*$_{i,t}$), presidential influence indicators—a vector of different expressions of the president's influence with Congress ($\hat{\beta_1}$ *Approval Rating*$_{i,t}$ + $\hat{\beta_2}$ *Whether the President Is a Lame Duck*$_{i,t}$), economic indicators—a vector of different expressions of the strength of the extant economy ($\hat{\beta_1}$ *Unemployment Rate*$_{i,t}$ + $\hat{\beta_2}$ *Inflation Rate*$_{i,t}$ + $\hat{\beta_3}$ *Recession*$_{i,t}$), as well as a control variable signifying whether or not there is divided government and a control variable regarding newspaper articles indicating the public's attention to the economy in the second model (M2).

Independent Variables

This analysis employed the digital *Public Papers of the President* in *The American Presidency Project*. Each economic speech, from 1948 through 2008, was searched for the trigger word "economy" to determine the "population." Thus, I coded and analyzed a total of 1,524 presidential speeches. As illustrated by table 5.1, the coding was focused on the tone (positivity, negativity) of presidential rhetoric; measuring rhetoric as political phenomena is commonly assessed this way in political science literature (Arthur and Woods, 2013; Baumgartner and Jones, 2009; Eshbaugh-Soha, 2006; Wood, 2007). Each presidential mention of the economy signaling Congress was coded with eleven variables.

Table 5.1. Example Sentences Exemplifying the Tone of Presidential Economic Rhetoric.

	Stratified Random Sample Speeches from The American Presidency Project
H. S. Truman 1/6/1947	As the year 1947 begins, the state of our national economy presents great opportunities for all. We have virtually full employment. Our national production of goods and services is 50 percent higher than in any year prior to the war emergency. The national income in 1946 was higher than in any peacetime year.
D. D. Eisenhower 1/6/1955	Second, to help keep our economy vigorous and expanding, thus sustaining our international strength and assuring better jobs, better living, better opportunities for every citizen;
J. F. Kennedy 5/8/1962	I do not believe that our tasks are done. There are proposals which we have put forward which we believe will be of assistance in moving this economy toward that full employment which all of Western Europe has achieved for over a period of fifteen years, and we are asking Congress for a program that will make this full employment a reality.
R. M. Nixon 4/26/1971	And, third, you can be confident that America's economy will continue its vigorous expansion without bringing on a new round of inflation.
R. W. Reagan 11/21/1987	In a moment I'd like to tell you about our efforts this past week to cut the federal deficit in order to keep the American economy growing and strong. First, though, I'd like to stress that very fact. Despite stock market fluctuations, despite all you may have heard to the contrary, the truth is: The American economy remains growing and strong.
W. J. Clinton 1/6/1995	This morning I am pleased to announce that the recovery of which our economic plan was such a large part has brought paychecks to more than a quarter million more Americans in December alone. And compared with an unemployment rate of over 7 percent when I took office, we now see an unemployment rate in December of 5.4 percent. We have grown the private economy as we have cut government. That's a real recovery and a real bargain for the American people.
G. W. Bush 2/8/2006	Our economy is strong, and it's getting stronger. We're now entering our fifth year of uninterrupted economic growth, and last year, our economy grew at a healthy 3.5 percent. Real after-tax income is up nearly 8 percent per American since 2001. Productivity growth is high. Small businesses are thriving. America has added 4.7 million new jobs over the last 2 1/2 years. The unemployment rate is down to 4.7 percent, the lowest level since July 2001.

Adapted from *The American Presidency Project*, 2014.

The coding included:

- The number of positive speeches
- The number of negative speeches
- Whether the economic rhetoric was in the first one hundred days of assuming office (1 = yes or 0 = no)
- The average monthly approval rating of the president
- Whether the rhetoric came while the president was a lame duck
- The number of presidential requests for economic legislation
- Whether or not there was divided government (1 = yes or 0 = no)
- The unemployment rate each month
- The inflation rate each month
- Whether or not there was a recession (1 = yes; 0 = no)
- The number of newspaper articles addressing the economy (*New York Times*)

Dependent Variables

I created two dependent variables from the *Policy Agendas Project* data. The outcome variable is dichotomous, wherein "1" represents either a congressional hearing in the first model (M1) and a public law in the second model (M2). The "0" will represent no congressional hearings during the time frame measured in the first model and no public laws in the second model. I excluded those hearings on the economy that had to do with appropriations and reauthorizations. Edwards and Wood (1999) argue that including such elements confuse the data and the results (p. 329).

Effect of Presidential Rhetoric on Congressional Economic Behavior

To find the probability that presidential tone could create changes in congressional hearings and public laws, I performed a negative binomial regression. Table 5.2 presents the coefficients, incident rate ratios, and *p*-values, as well as the percent changes in odds and the measures of fit for the regression analyses. Therefore, the substantive effects are as follows for the effect the rhetoric can have on the economic behavior of Congress, namely, hearings on the economy and economic legislation.

For the first model (M1), the hypotheses addressing the vector of presidential rhetoric are mostly in line with the theory. Pertaining to H1 and H2, the results indicate that the president's negative economic rhetoric has no impact upon the number of congressional hearings on the economy. Regard-

Table 5.2. Predicting Changes in Congressional Behavior Regarding the Economy.

	Dependent Variable: Pr (Success = # Hearings or 0 = No Hearings) N = 610			
	Policy Agendas Project Data on Congressional Hearings—(M1)			
	Coefficients	*Standard Errors*	*Factor Change*	*p-Values*
Positive Statements	−0.0352	0.0311	0.977	0.449
Negative Statements	−0.0316	0.0427	0.969	0.459
1st 100 Days in Office	0.0971	0.0611	1.10	0.112
Requests for Legislation	0.1057	0.0536	1.11	0.048
Approval Ratings	−0.0005	0.0032	0.999	0.881
"Lame Duck" President	−0.1643	0.1100	0.849	0.135
Unemployment Rate	0.2569	0.0253	1.29	0.000
Inflation Rate	0.0689	0.0119	1.07	0.000
Recession	−0.3268	0.0981	0.721	0.001
Divided Government	0.2016	0.0757	1.22	0.008
Log Likelihood – 1,382.13	$\chi^2 = 196.51$ ($p < 0.0000$)			

ing positive rhetoric, the results appear to be the same; positive economic rhetoric does not affect congressional hearings on the economy either. Assessing whether the tone of a president's rhetoric can motivate Congress appears to be the wrong approach.

Moreover, as in H6, petitions for economic actions in the first one hundred days in office did result in more congressional hearings, but the coefficient was indistinguishable from zero (see table 5.2). Interestingly in H3, however, the number of presidential requests for legislation did result in more congressional hearings on the economy. In other words, the more often a president requests that Congress produce economic legislation, the likelihood that there will be zero hearings is diminished. As illustrated by figure 5.3, the magnitude of the presidents' requests for legislation is quite miniscule in its ability to predict the increase in congressional hearings, however.

The hypotheses addressing the vector of presidential influence are mostly in-line with the theory (see table 5.2). Pertaining to H4 and H7, the results indicate higher presidential approval ratings have no bearing on congressional hearings on the economy. Moreover, the argument that Congress is responsive to presidents regarding the economy is not supported by these results; in fact, Congress is less likely to have hearings on the economy during

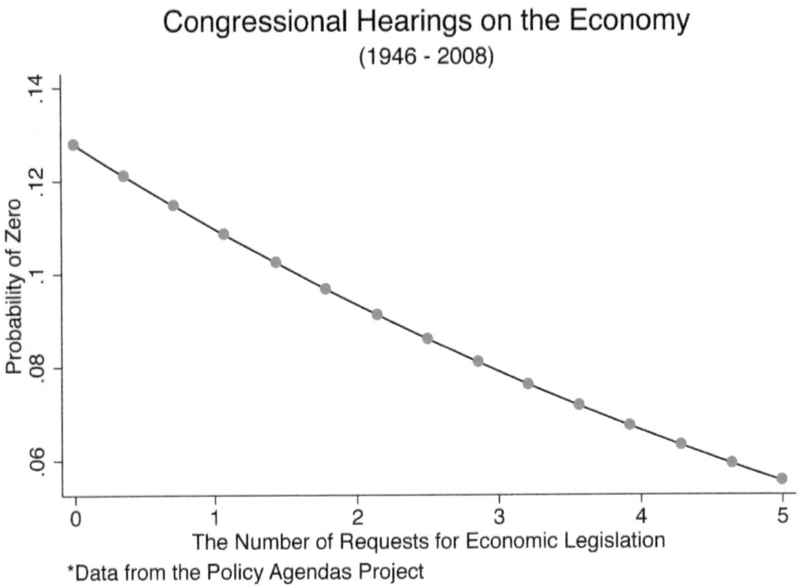

Figure 5.3. Presidential Requests for Economic Legislation.

presidential administrations that are considered lame ducks. It is more likely that lame duck presidents have less influence over congressional behavior.

I needed to consider how other potential correlates play into congressional behavior with regard to the economy in order to make sure the model was specified correctly and, more importantly, to identify other factors that influence Congress. Interestingly, the presence of divided government creates more congressional hearings on the economy. I would speculate that this has more to do with party dynamics, particularly opposite party politics wherein Congress is trying to call attention to the economy in the hopes that it reflects poorly on the president.

With regards to H8, H9, and H10, the results suggest that the economic indicators are a better predictor of congressional behavior than presidential rhetoric. The more negative the economy becomes, as in higher unemployment and inflation rates, Congress will have more hearings on the economy. Interestingly, however, is the result regarding the presence of a recession. There are fewer congressional hearings during recessions. One could speculate that there would be more of an attempt to correct the economic problems, yet the opposite seems to be true. Congress most likely does not want any negative attention regarding the economy so they do not discuss the economy when it is in a recession. In fact, these results are highly suggestive that Congress does respond to the negative economy, as illustrated by figure 5.4. As the theory argues, this result makes sense given the arguments in the literature; presidents rarely talk about the negative economy (Eshbaugh-Soha, 2010; Eshbaugh-Soha and Peake, 2005; Hoffman and Howard, 2010). Therefore, Congress wants to call attention to the economy because their constituency demands it. They do not need signals from the president to understand the situation. I could speculate that this result suggests that Congress is paying more attention to their own reelection, constituency demands, and historical legacy rather than the rhetoric of the president.

For the second model (M2), the hypotheses addressing the vector of presidential rhetoric are, again, mostly in line with the theory. Pertaining to H1 and H2, the results indicate that the president's negative economic rhetoric has no impact on the number of public laws that address the economy. Regarding positive rhetoric, the results appear to be the same; positive economic rhetoric does not affect public laws on the economy either. As illustrated by table 5.3, it is not more likely that the tone of the economic rhetoric will predict changes in congressional economic behavior. Congress does not

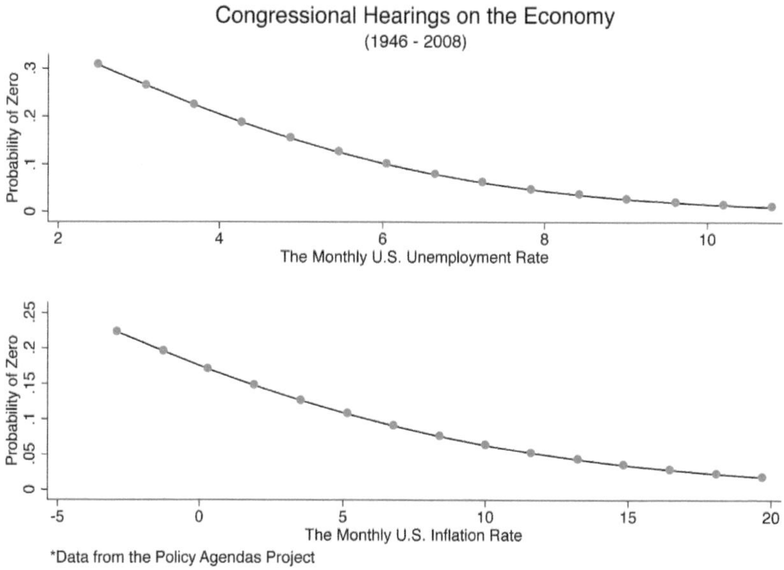

Figure 5.4. Economic Indicators and Congressional Behavior (M1).

send more bills that address the economy to the president to become public law as a result of the rhetoric. Interestingly in H3, however, the number of presidential requests for legislation resulted in fewer public laws on the economy (see table 5.3). In other words, the more often a president requests that Congress produce economic legislation, the likelihood that there will be zero bills is increased. This result confirms Kernell's (2007) analysis wherein he claims that going public keeps Congress from receiving the credit and the benefits from doing what was required. This creates direct opposition to the president's requests and engenders a contentious environment wherein the president gets less than he wants legislatively (Kernell, 2007).

The hypotheses addressing the vector of presidential influence are in-line with the theory (see table 5.3). Pertaining to H4 and H7, the results indicate higher presidential approval ratings have no bearing on public laws on the economy. Moreover, the argument that Congress is responsive to presidents is not supported by these results; in fact, Congress is less likely to produce economic legislation during presidential administrations that are considered lame ducks.

Interestingly, the presence of divided government has no statistically significant effect on the enaction of legislation that addresses on the economy; it was not very instrumental. The direction of the coefficient is correct,

Table 5.3. Predicting Changes in Congressional Behavior Regarding the Economy.

	Dependent Variable: Pr (Success = # Public Laws or 0 = No Hearings) N = 369			
	Policy Agendas Project Data on Public Laws—(M2)			
	Coefficients	*Standard Errors*	*Factor Change*	*p-Values*
Positive Statements	0.1038	0.0677	1.11	0.125
Negative Statements	0.0099	0.1211	1.01	0.934
1st 100 Days in Office	–0.1606	0.2571	0.852	0.532
Requests for Legislation	–0.3014	0.1546	0.740	0.051
Approval Ratings	0.0121	0.0097	1.01	0.211
"Lame Duck" President	0.3188	0.3447	1.38	0.355
Unemployment Rate	0.2605	0.0816	1.30	0.001
Inflation Rate	0.1929	0.0389	1.21	0.000
Recession	–0.3748	0.3224	0.869	0.245
Divided Government	–0.2852	0.2486	0.752	0.251
Newspaper Articles	0.0447	0.0214	1.05	0.037
	Log Likelihood – 310.44	$\chi^2 = 53.29$ ($p < 0.0000$)		

but it is indistinguishable from zero. I would speculate that this has to do with credit claiming, particularly each party trying to call attention to the economy in the way that reflects their self-interests.

With regard to H8, H9, and H10, the results suggest that the economic indicators are, mostly, a better predictor of congressional behavior than presidential rhetoric, as illustrated in figure 5.5. The more negative the economy becomes, as in higher unemployment and inflation rates, Congress will produce more bills on the economy. As in M1, these results are highly suggestive that Congress responds to the negative economy. As the theory argues, this result makes sense given the arguments in the literature (Eshbaugh-Soha, 2010; Eshbaugh-Soha and Peake, 2005; Hoffman and Howard, 2010). Therefore, Congress most likely wants to correct economic problems or circumstances because their constituency demands it and doing so will facilitate in their own reelection, constituency demands, and historical legacy. This can be seen in the newspaper articles variable; as attention to the economy grows in the public sphere, Congress is more likely to produce economic legislation showing their attention to the problem and their attention to the public.

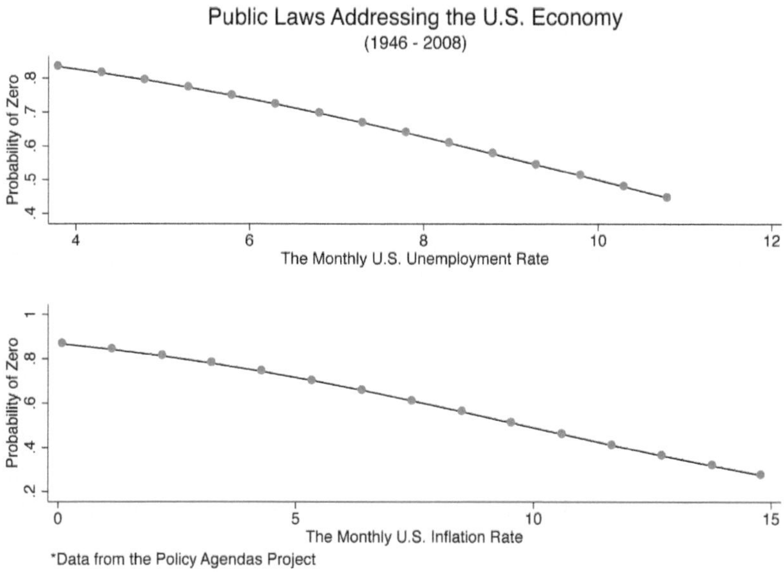

Figure 5.5. Economic Indicators and Congressional Behavior (M2)

Conclusion

The literature is overwhelmed with studies about what presidents do to try to accomplish specific actions with their rhetoric, even directing it to specific political actors. This extends to the tactics they take in order to become more successful in their policy objectives such as making veto threats about legislation that they do not want to see become law, going public with their own requests for making legislation, and trying to build coalitions of policy elites as well as actions they take to make their approval ratings higher.

There are instances wherein it appears that rhetorical cues and signals presidents send to Congress worked. It is anecdotal evidence, however, which shows how presidents use their rhetorical cues and signals to convince Congress to support certain policy goals. For instance, President Roosevelt used radio programing that he called "Fireside Chats" to garner support for his economic policy programs. On the surface, it seems that his plan was successful. Moreover, President Johnson "went public" with Civil Rights rhetoric in the hopes of convincing the public as well as Congress that changes were necessary. Again, it seemed to have worked. However, the same cannot be said with President Carter and his attempt to go public with the energy package. His rhetoric did not accomplish what he wanted (Light, 1999).

It is difficult to find data or systematic studies that prove presidential rhetoric can be used consistently to garner support. The research is not comprehensive. This study sought to contribute to the research and offer a more comprehensive perspective regarding presidential rhetoric's effect. The results from these hypotheses suggest that rhetoric is not successful in influencing Congress's economic behavior. Congressional actions on the economy seem to respond to external elements such as existing economic conditions rather than positive or negative presidential economic rhetoric. The aforementioned analysis indicates that the president is not the most important or even the central actor in economic policy (Pack, 1988).

The lack of significance in predicting changes to congressional behavior is telling from a "rhetoric as a mechanism of influence" perspective. It is more likely that members of Congress are paying attention to the economy, its indicators, and their own reelection prospects (via their constituency demands) than it is that they are paying attention to the rhetoric of the presidents. The economic rhetoric does not create an impetus for action, but rather it is too constrained by the externalities of Congress and the powers it possesses.

Notes

1. The purpose of going public is not simply to offer policies and programs to the public to garner support from the people, but to motivate the public to contact their members of Congress about the policy. This activity is intended to make the economic agenda of the president the agenda of Congress, via its constituencies. Going public is an attempt to give the president more legislative influence and to help him accomplish his economic goals by pressuring Congress (Kernell, 2007).

2. There are political realities that decrease the president's influence in Congress. Changes in economic indicators such as unemployment, inflation, and the deficit create serious conflict between the president and Congress (Peterson, 1990). Presidents, however employ specific tactics that they think will help them be more successful at increasing their influence with Congress. They make veto threats about legislation that they do not want to see become law. They go public with their own requests for legislation. They try to build coalitions of policy elites. They even try to make their approval ratings higher.

3. Saeki and Shull (2003) argue that Congress uses its power to call hearings to influence how and to what extent the Fed alters monetary policy. Beck (1982) claims that the Fed responds to these cues from Congress for fear that Congress will alter the Fed's independent agency status. Havrilesky (1995) argues that Congress exercises a significant influence over the Federal Funds Rate (FFR) when it communicates its policy preferences in the biannual Congressional Oversight Hearings on monetary policy. Morris and Munger (1998) argue that the Fed will not choose policies opposed by Congress. Moreover, Waller (1992) argues that the Senate, through the confirmation process, can prevent particular appointees from joining the Fed Board. Each of these actions and approaches enables Congress to influence monetary policy, which has consequential effects on the U.S. economy.

Conclusion

> It is true that you may fool all of the people some of the time; you can even fool some of the people all the time; but you can't fool all of the people all the time.
>
> —Abraham Lincoln (Woolley and Peters, 2014 —"Ronald Regan, 1985")

This research contributes to the discussion about the expectations of the Office of the Presidency and presidential intentions for using rhetoric to garner influence over the economy and its most important actors. These expectations have been rising even as the president's capacity to meet them has been declining, and the increased expectations have created difficulties for presidents. It must be said, however, that presidents are partly to blame for the heightened expectations. They promise more to the people because expectations of what the president can do for the public are high. The public's refusal to understand the limitations of what the president is able to do compels presidents to increase their promises. Presidents have an incentive to meet these expectations because they are considered great presidents if history deems that they have done so and marginal if they are unsuccessful. It is a cyclical activity in which presidents engage.

Presidential expectations for the economy have evolved gradually over time. According to Corwin (1958) and Tulis (1987), the expectations of the president were drastically different prior to the New Deal than they are for modern presidents (Tulis, 1987). Since that time, the presidency has undergone a major institutional change, with this shift occurring because of how presidents use rhetoric (Tulis, 1987). They now utilize their rhetoric to foster support for their economic agendas, which they now have because they are expected to have them.

The public expects the president to do something about every aspect of the economy—but the public has different expectations for each president (Neustadt, 1991). These expectations are conditioned by the current *sitz im leben* or the context in which they live—primarily the state of the economy, public support, and a coalition of like-minded congresspersons (Mondak, Mutz, and Huckfeldt, 1996). Each president is judged according to his ability to meet those expectations before he leaves office. Moreover, the expectations can change depending on a number of factors.

The president's responsibilities regarding the economy have increased, but his ability to meet those demands has decreased (Light, 1999; Edwards and Wayne, 1985). The expectations for the economy increase with every new president because of the previous president and the promises he made. The problem, however, is that the president is quite limited in terms of what he can do about the economy. These limited capabilities create a serious predicament for the president. The support from his constituencies dwindles unless he can meet their expectations.

They have promised to do more and more for the economy to appear more effective and powerful as economic leaders; yet, those promises create an opportunity for their constituencies to hold them accountable. If they are unable to meet the expectations they established, they look ineffectual. Thus, presidents weaken the Office of the Presidency by their increased promises and by their inability to achieve results. Now the public expects more from presidents with regard to the economy, creating impetus for the cycle of increasing expectations and decreasing influence (Light, 1999).

It is commonly argued that presidential power is the power to persuade and/or bargain, and presidential rhetoric is an extension, or rather a mechanism, of that power. Rhetoric is one way that presidents try to assert their power and position over other political actors, the public, and institutions. To be effective at asserting their power, however, presidents must appeal to the most pertinent economic actors. Using the most commonly argued mechanism of presidential power and persuasion, namely presidential rhetoric, are they successful?

Presidents want to shape monetary policy, the regulation of the supply of money, the unemployment rate, and the inflation rate. Doing so enables them to look effective as a leader, shape U.S. policy for decades, and secure a place in history with a lasting legacy as well as solidify their reelection, in most cases. However, the president's capacity to control economic policy is a point of much contention. The political realities of the president's relationship with the Federal Reserve (Fed) and the limitations the relationship imposes on the president make it difficult for him to fulfill his promises. This book has presented data and analyses suggesting that neither positive nor negative economic rhetoric from the president is able to predict the probability that the Fed will change the Federal Funds Rate (FFR) to meet the requests of the president.

Moreover, scholars argue that presidents have been trying to influence the public since the inception of the modern presidency (Edwards, 2003; Tulis, 1987; Wood, 2007). My findings suggest that voters' perceptions of the economy come from their party ideologies and from their personal experiences with the economy rather than from the positive speeches of the president. This element of the research adds another perspective to the literature on presidential economic rhetoric and expands the discussion.

Lastly, presidents typically try to influence Congress to follow their economic policy goals (Canes-Wrone, 2001; Edwards, 1995). This research, however, provides results that suggest members of Congress are not passively waiting for the president to lead them on economic policy, be it fiscal or monetary. My results indicate that members of Congress are concerned with their own versions of "good policy" and their own reelection, which often leads them in a different direction, economically, from the president (Fenno, 1978; Mayhew, 1989; Jacobs and Shapiro, 2000). More specifically, presidential success comes from external elements, such as party coalitions, unified government, and existing economic indicators as well as historical context and a bit of luck. Despite presidential attempts to tailor rhetoric to effect results, they are unsuccessful on this front, in nearly every way. In short, the statistical results of this study suggest that some research might have overstated the claims about presidential power as internally based (Neustadt, 1990; Wood, 2007). Alternatively, it seems as though a more realistic assessment of presidential power would consider more closely the external limitations that confine presidential will (Light, 1999).

Presidents can attempt to use their rhetoric to effect changes; however, they are not going to be successful if the policy window is closed, the external resources are unavailable, and the economic actors have no self-interested reason to accommodate the president's requests (Kingdon, 1995; Light, 1999). Additionally, different presidents face vastly different environments wherein they are trying to persuade economic actors (Mondak, Mutz, and Huckfeldt, 1996). The economic situations and the political environments that presidents find themselves in are not equal to one another (Sigelman and Rosenblatt, 1996). Therefore, attempting to determine the "success" of direct influence of presidential rhetoric over the economy is the wrong approach to studying presidential rhetoric.

Most importantly scholarship has to address why presidents spend so much of their time giving speeches when research suggests that presidential rhetoric is not an effective mechanism of presidential power. Maybe presidents have to engage in rhetorical activity to maintain some semblance of strength so that they do not look weak or ineffectual. It is possible that presidents think they could be effective with their rhetoric if they were able to provide a narrative with which the public could relate and identify—after all, they did this during whatever campaign they won. Nevertheless, these queries need to be answered or at least represent an area that requires further inquiry and discussion. Rhetoric scholarship needs to substantially modify its approach to presidential rhetoric if it is to continue as a legitimate approach within presidential rhetoric studies. It needs to find a better way of classifying presidential rhetoric or clearly differentiating between the various classifications of rhetoric, such as crisis rhetoric, agenda-setting rhetoric, and symbolic rhetoric.

Future Directions of Presidential Economic Rhetoric Research

Given the findings presented here, the basic theories of this research could be extended to further contribute to the literature and the discipline. I believe there are many different justifiable directions that the research could take. Most importantly, I think that this could be accomplished by including more variations of presidential rhetoric in the model. The prevalence of the "permanent presidential campaign" and the "governing-by-campaigning" approach necessitate study of the environment that the permanent campaign creates. Presidents govern as though they are campaigning, which enables them to have an entourage of staff members who saturate the talking-heads shows and the Sunday talk shows and respond to and speak about the president's economic messages. Therefore, the messages that presidents are trying to convey to economic actors are mostly consistent and often are presented by actors other than the president. It would be worth considering whether this extension of the definition of presidential rhetoric makes a substantive difference in the behaviors of economic actors. Extending the definition of presidential rhetoric to include other presidential actors would expand the audiences that the president is able to reach. As Wood (2007) and Eshbaugh-Soha (2006) argue, the president should be able to saturate the conversation with his economic perspective, and increasing the number of people that the president's rhetoric reaches would potentially create more opportunity for the rhetoric to shape behavior.

Such research would have to include a substantive theoretical justification for considering rhetoric that comes from a governmental actor who is not the president and then treating that rhetoric as though it is "presidential rhetoric" for whatever analysis is undertaken. I am aware that this extension could be considered a change to the very definition of "presidential rhetoric." Essentially, I would be asking "what is presidential rhetoric?" Would it be considered only instances where the president talks, or does it extend to cases where the public hears rhetoric from the most trusted presidential economic advisors and administrators? This rhetoric is presented by trusted economic actors at the president's direction and seeks to advance the president's message with specific actors and audiences. However, if rhetoric is everything, then rhetoric is nothing. Moreover, there is a reason we study presidential rhetoric as it comes from an individual who is typically dynamic, charismatic, inspiring as well as doing the nearly impossible, namely, obtaining a national constituency.

Nevertheless, I think that there exists a rational justification for extending the definition of rhetoric. We know, from many facets of research, that the president's individual speeches are not able to change public opinion or motivate other government players to action. The surrogates have access, in many cases, to the economic actors the president is trying to reach. If their rhetoric matches the rhetoric of the president, it is worth determining whether or not the economic actors respond to this rhetoric differently than they respond to the president's rhetoric. In other words, are the trusted presidential surrogates able to more definitively narrativize the president's messages? Extending the definition of rhetoric to include presidential surrogates, particularly the Council of Economic Advisors (CEA), the Department of the Treasury, and the Office of Management and Budget (OMB) as well as the president's Senior Policy Advisors, may offer insights into how the bureaucracy, the public, and Congress respond to the presidents and their economic plans.

Understanding this *economic subpresidency*'s effect is crucial for the larger picture of the study of presidential rhetoric (Anderson, 1999). It will help ascertain if presidents are able to influence the actions of some of the actors closest to them by determining if the rhetoric from trusted economic officials, appointed by the president, matches the tone of the president's rhetoric. Including those actors who are nearly a direct extension of the president and his rhetoric in the economic subpresidency would provide a better model of presidential rhetoric addressing the economy and economic policy, particularly because it expands the president's audience.

In addition, an analysis that incorporates the use of social media like Facebook and Twitter would be important to understanding presidential rhetoric. Future presidents are going to use social media more often, largely because of the precedent set by Barack Obama. Social media outlets seem to be more effective mechanisms for presenting their messages.[1] Presidents are able to control the content and tone of the message, completely bypassing the biases of the print media and television. Moreover, social media allows for an expansion of their constituencies. For instance, President Obama has over 42 million Twitter followers and nearly 40 million Facebook friends. This totaling of his massive following and unhindered direct connection to the public does not even include the 12 million Facebook friends and 5 million Twitter followers his wife has or those of the countless other supporters who can and do communicate with the public at his specific direction.

Furthermore, he has daily contact with these individuals, which is drastically different from trying to utilize television to connect with the public. The president can garner about 40 million viewers during his State of the Union Addresses, but he can only do so once a year for a brief period of time, if they are watching. President Obama can reach double that number of people every day with the use of social media. Even assuming some overlap between social media users and television viewers, he still has tremendous access to a massive audience.

It is noteworthy to mention, as Edwards (2003) points out, that the majority of the public cannot remember a single point the president has discussed in any given speech (p. 208). Therefore, research that addresses how effective the president is in using Twitter and Facebook to communicate his message and motivate the public through social media is essential for the future of presidential rhetoric studies. Is social media a more effective method of "going public" or garnering influence for presidents? Moreover, is it materially the same as the more traditional forms of rhetoric that have been studied in the existing literature? Again, this is a different aspect of presidential rhetoric—written communication. Does "hearing" the president's voice make a difference? Furthermore, this is especially important with the onslaught of television companies like Netflix and Amazon Prime. It is not unreasonable to assume that as cable television changed presidential communication strategies, these "a la carte" TV watching programs could change the way presidents communicate in the future.

This research could be conducted using Hopkins and King's (2010) work on *automated nonparametric content analysis* of blog posts. This methodological approach could be employed to determine the tone of the tweets and the Facebook posts. Hopkins and King (2010) use content analysis to ascertain the tone of digital texts (blog posts). Their created *R* program codes the entire text with a tone of either –2 (extremely negative), –1 (negative), 0 (neutral), 1 (positive), or 2 (extremely positive). However, such research, while valuable, would be a formidable undertaking and quite complex in nature.

Coda

Considering this research, it seems that the president's decision to address the economy so often must stem from a symbolic placation or institutional necessity that is intended to comfort constituencies or somehow garner electoral advocacy from the party's base. No other viable explanation really exists given the lack of results presidents obtain from discussing the economy and, on the other hand, their persistent determination to do so. This discrepancy leads me to believe that presidential rhetoric on the economy is, at best, a tool presidents use to appear concerned about the economy to everyone and toeing the party-line to their base. Moreover, it allows them to present the facade, to their constituents, that they are in control of an important facet of American life, the state of the country's economy. The truth is that we need a strong economy to maintain our Democracy; not many would deny this reality. Thus, presidents naturally want to present themselves as participants in the perpetuation of American democracy because if they fail to do so, they risk being judged harshly by the public and, more importantly, by history.

Note

1. See the work of James Fowler and others on how activities on Facebook can increase voter turnout at www.nature.com/nature/journal/v489/n7415/abs/nature11421.html.

References

Abramowitz, A. (2008). "Forecasting the 2008 Presidential Election with the Time-for-Change Model." *PS: Political Science and Politics*, Issue 4 (October): 691–695.

Abrams, B. A. (2006). "How Richard Nixon Pressured Arthur Burns: Evidence from the Nixon Tapes." *Journal of Economic Perspectives*, vol. 20, no. 4: 177–188.

Aldrich, J. H., and D. W. Rohde (2000). "The Consequences of Party Organization in the House: The Role of the Majority and Minority Parties in Conditional Party Government." In *Polarized Politics: Congress and the President in a Partisan Era* edited by J. Bond and R. Fleisher. Washington, DC: Congressional Quarterly Press.

American National Election Studies (2008). (www.electionstudies.org). *The ANES Guide to Public Opinion and Electoral Behavior*. Ann Arbor: University of Michigan, Center for Political Studies [producer and distributor].

Anderson, J. (1999). "Economic Policy: Comparative Advisory Arrangements." In Steven A. Shull's *Presidential Policymaking: An End-of-Century Assessment*. Armonk, NY: M.E. Sharpe.

———. (1993). "Managing Macroeconomic Policy: The Carter Experience." In *The Presidency Reconsidered*, edited by R. W. Waterman, 247–273. Itasca, IL: F. E. Peacock.

Arnold, R. D. (1990). *The Logic of Congressional Action*. New Haven, CT: Yale University Press.

Arthur, C. D., and Woods, J. (2013). "The Contextual Presidency: The Negative Shift in Presidential Immigration Rhetoric." *Presidential Studies Quarterly*, vol. 43, no. 3 (September): 468–489.

Aune, J. A. (2008). "The Econo-Rhetorical Presidency." In *The Prospect of Presidential Rhetoric*, edited by J. A. Aune and M. J. Medhurst, 46–68. College Station: Texas A&M University Press.

Aune, J. A., and Medhurst, M. J. (Eds.) (2008). *The Prospect of Presidential Rhetoric*. College Station: Texas A&M University Press.

Auerbach, R. D. (1985). "Politics and the Federal Reserve." *Contemporary Policy Issues*, vol. 3, no. 5 (Fall): 43–58.

Bachrach, P., and Baratz, M. (1962). "The Two Faces of Power." *American Political Science Review*, vol. 56: 947–952.

Barabas, J. (2008). "Presidential Policy Initiatives: How the Public Learns about State of the Union Proposals from the Mass Media." *Presidential Studies Quarterly*, vol. 38: 195–222.

Barrett, A. W. (2005). "Going Public as a Legislative Weapon: Measuring Presidential Appeals Regarding Specific Legislation." *Presidential Studies Quarterly*, vol. 35: 1–10.

———. (2004). "Gone Public: The Impact of Going Public on Presidential Legislative Success." *American Politics Research*, vol. 32, no. 3: 338–370.

Barrett A. W., and Eshbaugh-Soha M. (2007). "Presidential Success on the Substance of Legislation." *Political Research Quarterly*, vol. 60: 100–112.

Bartlett, B. (2004). "(More) Politics at the Fed? Greenspan Should Tighten A.S.A.P.—For His and the Country's Good." *National Review Online*. Accessed at: www.nationalreview.com/articles/210446/more-politics-fed/bruce-bartlett.

Baum, M. A. (2004). "Going Private: Public Opinion, Presidential Rhetoric, and the Domestic Politics of Audience Costs in U.S. Foreign Policy Crises." *Journal of Conflict Resolution*, vol. 48, no. 5: 603–631.

Baum, M., and Groeling, T. (2008). "New Media and the Polarization of American Political Discourse." *Political Communication*, Issue 23: 345–365.

———. (2005). "What Gets Covered? How Media Coverage of Elite Debate Drives the Rally-'Round-the-Flag Phenomenon: 1979–1998." In *Public Domain: Presidents and the Challenges of Public Leadership*, edited by L. C. Han and D. J. Heith, 71–106. Albany: State University of New York Press.

Baum, M., and Kernell, S. (1999). "Has Cable Ended the Golden Age of Presidential Television?" *American Political Science Review*, vol. 93, no. 1: 99–114.

Baumgartner, F., and Jones, B. D. (2009). *Agendas and Instability in American Politics*. Chicago: University of Chicago Press.

Baumgartner, F. R., Jones, B. D., and Leech, B. L. (1997). "Media Attention and Congressional Agendas." In *Do the Media Govern? Politicians, Voters, and Reporters in America*, edited by S. Iyengar and R. Reeves, 349–363. Thousand Oak, CA: Sage.

Beck, M. S. (2009). "The Economy, Obama, and the 2008 Election: Editor's Introduction." *PS: Political Science and Politics*, vol 42.3 (July 2009): 479–483.

Beck, N. (1987). "Elections and the Fed: Is There a Political Monetary Cycle?" *American Journal of Political Science*, vol. 31: 194–214.

———. (1982). "Presidential Influence on the Federal Reserve in the 1970s." *American Journal of Political Science*, vol. 26, no. 3 (August): 415–445.

Behr, R., and Iyengar, S. (1985). "Television News, Real-World Cues, and Change in the Public Agenda." *Public Opinion Quarterly*, vol. 49: 38–57.

Bligh, M. C., Kohles, J. C., and Meindl, J. R. (2004). "Charisma Under Crisis: Presidential Leadership, Rhetoric, and Media Responses before and after the September 11th Terrorist Attacks," *Leadership Quarterly*, vol. 15, no. 2: 211–239.

Bond, J., and Fleisher, R. (2000a). "Polarized Politics: Does It Matter?" In *Polarized Politics: Congress and the President in a Partisan Era*, edited by J. Bond and R. Fleisher, 186–200. Washington, DC: Congressional Quarterly Press.

———. (2000b). "Congress and the President in a Partisan Era." In *Polarized Politics: Congress and the President in a Partisan Era*, edited by J. Bond and R. Fleisher, 1–8. Washington, DC: Congressional Quarterly Press.

———. (1990). *The President in the Legislative Arena.* Chicago, IL: University of Chicago Press.

Bostdorff, D. M. (1994). *The Presidency and the Rhetoric of Foreign Crisis.* Columbia: University of South Carolina Press.

Boydstun, Glazier, and Pietryka. (2013). "Playing to the Crowd: Agenda Control in Presidential Debates." *Political Communication*, Vol. 30, no. 2: 254–277.

Brace, P., and Hinckley, B. (1992). *Follow the Leader: Opinion Polls and the Modern Presidency*. New York: Basic Books.

Brady, D. W., and Volden, C. (2006). *Revolving Gridlock.* Boulder, CT: Westview Press.

Brambor, T., Clark, W., and Golder, M. (2006). "Understanding Interaction Models: Improving Empirical Analyses." *Political Analysis*, vol. 14, no. 1: 63–82.

Brehm, J., and Gates, S. (1997). *Working, Shirking, and Sabotage: Bureaucratic Response to a Democratic Public.* Ann Arbor: University of Michigan Press.

Brody, R. A. (1991). *Assessing the President: The Media, Elite Opinion, and Public Support.* Stanford, CA: Stanford University Press.

Burden, B. C., and Sanberg, J. N. R. (2003). "Budget Rhetoric in Presidential Campaigns from 1952 to 2000." *Political Behavior*, vol. 25: 97–118.

Campbell, J., Evans, C., Fisher, J., and Justiniano, A. (2012). "Macroeconomic Effects of FOMC Forward Guidance." Working paper, Federal Reserve Bank of Chicago.

Cameron, C. (2000). *Veto Bargaining: Presidents and the Politics of Negative Power.* New York: Cambridge University Press.

Canes-Wrone, B. (2006). *Who Leads Whom? Presidents, Policy, and the Public.* Chicago: University of Chicago Press.

———. (2004). "The Public Presidency, Personal Approval Ratings, and Policy Making." *Presidential Studies Quarterly*, vol. 34, no. 3: 477–490.

———. (2001). "The President's Legislative Influence from Public Appeals." *American Journal of Political Science*, vol. 45: 313–329.

Canes-Wrone, B., and de Marchi, S. (2002). "Presidential Approval and Legislative Success." *Journal of Politics*, vol. 64, no. 2: 491–509.

Carpini, M. X. D., and Keeter, S. (1996). *What Americans Know about Politics and Why It Matters.* New Haven, CT: Yale University Press.

Cavalli, C. D. (2006). *Presidential Legislative Activity: Using Quantifiable Measures to Explore Leadership in the American System.* Lanham, MD: University Press of America, Inc.

Chang, K. H. (2001). "The President Versus the Senate: Federal Open Market Committee (FOMC)." *Journal of Law, Economics, and Organization*, vol. 17, no. 2: 319–355. Oxford University Press.

Chappel, H., Havrilesky, T., and McGregor, R. (1993). "Partisan Monetary Policies: Presidential Influence Through the Power of Appointment." *Quarterly Journal of Economics*, vol. 108: 185–219.

Chong, D. (1996). "Creating Common Frames of Reference on Political Issues." In *Political Persuasion and Attitude Change*, edited by D. C. Mutz, P. M. Sniderman, and R. A. Brody, 195–224. Ann Arbor: University of Michigan Press.

Cohen, J. (2010). *Going Local: Presidential Leadership in the Post-Broadcast Age*. New York: Cambridge University Press.

———. (2008). *The Presidency in the Era of 24-Hour News*. Princeton, NJ: Princeton University Press.

———. (2004). "If the News Is so Bad, Why Are Presidential Polls so High? Presidents, the News Media, and the Mass Public in an Era of New Media." *Presidential Studies Quarterly*, vol. 34, no. 3, (September): 493–515.

Cohen, J. E. (1995). "Presidential Rhetoric and the Public Agenda." *American Journal of Political Science*, vol. 39 (February): 87–107.

Cohen, J. E., and Hamman, J. A. (2005). "Presidential Ideology and the Public Mood: 1956–1994." In *Public Domain: Presidents and the Challenges of Public Leadership*, edited by L. C. Han and D. J. Heith, 141–162. Albany: State University of New York Press.

———. (2003). "The Polls: Can Presidential Rhetoric Affect the Public's Economic Perceptions?" *Presidential Studies Quarterly*, vol. 33: 408–423.

Comiskey, M., and Marsh, L. (2012). "Presidents, Parties, and the Business Cycle, 1949–2009." *Presidential Studies Quarterly*, vol. 42, no. 1: 40–59.

Conley, R. (2002). *The Presidency, Congress, and Divided Government: A Post-War Assessment*. College Station: Texas A&M University Press.

Converse, P. (1964). "The Nature of Belief Systems in Mass Publics." In *Ideology and Discontent*, edited by David Apter, 206–261. New York: Free Press.

———. (1962). "Information Flow and the Stability of Partisan Attitudes." *Public Opinion Quarterly*, vol. 26: 578–599.

Corwin, E. S. (1958). *The President: Office and Powers*, 4th Revised Edition. New York: New York University Press.

Covington, C. R. (1987). "'Staying private': Gaining Congressional Support for Unpublicized Presidential Preferences on Roll Call Votes." *Journal of Politics*, vol. 49: 737–755.

Cox, G., and McCubbins, M. (2007). *Legislative Leviathan: Party Government in the House*. Berkeley: University of California Press.

Cunion, W. (2005). "Second-Term Presidents: Free Birds or Lame Ducks?" In *Public Domain: Presidents and the Challenges of Public Leadership*, edited by L. C. Han and D. J. Heith, 113–140. Albany: State University of New York Press.

Dahl, R. A. (1957). "The Concept of Power." *Behavioral Science*, vol. 2: 201–215

De Landtsheer, C., and Feldman, L. (Eds.). (2000). *Beyond Public Speech and Symbols: Explorations in the Rhetoric of Politicians and the Media*. Westport, CT: Praeger Publishers.

DiClerico, R. E. (2000). *The American President*, 5th Edition. Upper Saddle River, NJ: Prentice Hall Inc.

———. (1993). "The Role of Media in Heightened Expectations and Diminished Leadership Capacity." In *The Presidency Reconsidered*, edited by R. W. Waterman, 115–143. Itasca, IL: F. E. Peacock.

Doherty, D. (2008). "Presidential Rhetoric, Candidate Evaluation, and Party Identification: Can Parties 'Own' Values?" *Political Research Quarterly*, vol. 61, no. 3 (September): 419–433.

Dolan, C., Frendreis, J., and Tatalovich, R. (2008). *The Presidency and Economic Policy*. New York: Rowman and Littlefield.

Downs, A. (1967). *Inside Bureaucracy*. Long Grove, IL: Waveland Press, Inc.

Druckman, J. N., and Holmes, J. W. (2004). "Does Presidential Rhetoric Matter? Priming and Presidential Approval." *Presidential Studies Quarterly*, vol. 34: 755–777.

Durham, B., Wood, D., Owens, C., and Brandy, M. (2005). "Presidential Rhetoric and the Economy." Paper presented at the annual meeting of the American Political Science Association, Boston Marriott Copley Place, Boston, MA.

Edwards III, G. C. (2009). *The Strategic President: Persuasion and Opportunity in Presidential Leadership*. Princeton, NJ: Princeton University Press.

———. (2003). *On Deaf Ears: The Limits of the Bully Pulpit*. New Haven, CT: Yale University Press.

———. (2000). "Presidential Pulpit: Bully or Baloney?" In *Understanding the Presidency*, 2nd Edition, edited by James P. Pfiffner and Roger P. Davidson. New York: Longman.

———. (1996). "Presidential Rhetoric: What Difference Does It Make?" In *Beyond the Rhetorical Presidency*, edited by M. J. Medhurst, 199–217. College Station: Texas A&M University Press.

———. (1995). "Predicting Presidential Decision-Making from Presidential Language and Mass Media Reportage." *Presidential Studies Quarterly*, vol. 25: 43–65.

———. (1983). *The Public Presidency*. New York: St. Martin's Press.

———. (1980). *Presidential Influence in Congress*. San Francisco, CA: W. H. Freeman.

Edwards III, G. C., and Barrett, A. (2000a). "Presidential Agenda Setting in Congress." In *Polarized Politics: Congress and the President in a Partisan Era*, edited by Jon Bond and Richard Fleisher, 158–167. Washington, DC: Congressional Quarterly Press.

———. (2000b). "Presidential Agenda Setting in Congress." In *Polarized Politics: Congress and the President in a Partisan Era*, edited by Jon Bond and Richard Fleisher, 109–133. Washington, DC: Congressional Quarterly Press.

Edwards III, G. C., and Wayne, S. (1985). *Presidential Leadership: Politics and Policy Making*. New York: St. Martin's Press Inc.

Edwards III, G. C., and Wood, D. (1999). "Who Influences Whom? The President, Congress, and the Media." *American Political Science Review*, vol. 93, no. 2: 327–344.

Edwards, J. L. (2004). "Echoes of Camelot: How Images Construct Cultural Memory through Rhetorical Framing." In *Defining Visual Rhetorics*, edited by C. A. Hill and M. Helmers, 179–194. Mahwah, NJ: Lawrence Erlbaum Associates, Inc.

Eisner, M. (2000). *Regulatory Politics in Transition*. Baltimore, MD: Johns Hopkins University Press.

Ellis, R. J. (1998). *Speaking to the People: The Rhetorical Presidency in Historical Perspective*. Amherst: University of Massachusetts Press.

Eshbaugh-Soha, M. (2010a). "The Tone of Local Presidential News Coverage." *Political Communication*, vol. 27: 121–140.

———. (2010b). "How Policy Conditions the Impact of Presidential Speeches on Legislative Success." *Social Science Quarterly*, vol. 91, no.2 415–435.

———. (2010c). "The Politics of Presidential Speeches." *Congress and the Presidency*, vol. 37: 1–21.

———. (2008a). "The Impact of Presidential Speeches on the Bureaucracy." *Social Science Quarterly*, vol. 89 (March): 116–132.

———. (2008b). "Local newspaper coverage of the presidency." *International Journal of Press/Politics*, vol. 13: 103–119.

———. (2006). *The President's Speeches: Beyond "Going Public."* Boulder, CO: Lynne Rienner Publishers.

———. (2005). "Presidential Signaling in a Market Economy." *Presidential Studies Quarterly*, vol. 35, no. 4: 718.

Eshbaugh-Soha, M., and Peake, J. (2011). *Breaking through the Noise: Presidential Leadership, Public Opinion, and the News Media*. Standford, CA: Stanford University Press.

———. (2008). "The Presidency and Local Media: Local Newspaper Coverage of President George W. Bush." *Presidential Studies Quarterly*, vol. 38, no. 4: 609–631.

———. (2006). "The Contemporary Presidency: 'Going Local' to Reform Social Security." *Presidential Studies Quarterly*, vol. 36: 689–704.

———. (2005). "Presidents and the Economic Agenda." *Political Research Quarterly*, vol. 58, no. 1 (March): 127–138.

———. (2004). "Presidential Influence over the Systemic Agenda." *Congress and the Presidency*, vol. 31 (Autumn): 181–201.

Farnsworth, S. J., and Lichter, S. R.(2005). *The Mediated Presidency: Television News and Presidential Governance*. Lanham, MD: Rowman and Littlefield Publishing.

Fenno Jr., R. F. (1978). *Home Style: House Members in Their Districts*. Boston: Little, Brown.

Frances, M. F., Sorensen, T., and Gottheimer, J. (2010). *Power in Words: The Stories behind Barack Obama's Speeches, from the State House to the White House*. Boston: Beacon Press.

Frendreis, J., and Tatalovich, R. (1994). *The Modern Presidency and Economic Policy*. Itasca, IL: F. E. Peacock Publishers.

Friedrich, R. J. (1982). "In Defense of Multiplicative Terms in Multiple Regression Equations." *American Journal of Political Science*, vol. 26: 797–833.

Frumkin, N. (2004). *Guide to Economic Indicators*. Armonk, NY: M. E. Sharpe Publishers.

Galbraith, J. K. (1981). *A Life in Our Times*. New York: Ballantine Books.

Gallup Economy. (2014). www.gallup.com/poll/economy.aspx.

Gentzkow, M., and Shapiro, J. M. (2006). "Media Bias and Reputation." *Journal of Political Economy*, vol. 114: 280–316.

Gerring, J., Thacker, S., and Moreno, C. (2005). "Centripetal Democratic Governance: A Theory and Global Inquiry." *American Political Science Review*, vol. 99, no. 4 (November): 567–581.

Glazier, R. A., and A. E. Boydstun. (2012). "The President, the Press, and the War: A Tale of Two Framing Agendas." *Political Communication*, vol. 29, no. 4: 428–446.

Golden, D. G., and Poterba, J. H. (1980). "The Price of Popularity: The PBC Reexamined." *American Journal of Political Science*, vol. 24: 696–714.

Golden, M. (2000). *What Motivates Bureaucrats? Politics and Administration during the Reagan Years*. New York: Columbia University Press.

Gordon, R. J. (1990). "What Is New-Keynesian Economics?" *Journal of Economic Literature*, vol. 28, no. 3: 1115–1171.

Gormley, W. T. (1989). *Taming the Bureaucracy: Muscles, Prayers, and Other Strategies*. Princeton, NJ: Princeton University Press.

Graber, D. (2009). *Mass Media and American Politics*. Washington, DC: Congressional Quarterly Press.

Green, D. (1987). *Shaping Political Consciousness: The Language of Politics in America from McKinley to Reagan*. Ithaca, NY: Cornell University Press.

Groeling, T. (2008). "Who's the Fairest of Them All? An Empirical Test for Partisan Bias on ABC, CBS, NBC, and Fox News." *Presidential Studies Quarterly*, vol. 38, no. 4 (December): 631–657.

Gronke, P., and Miller, P. (2012). "Voting by Mail and Turnout in Oregon: Revisiting Southwell and Burchett." *American Politics Research*, vol. 40, no. 6: 976–997.

Hallin, D. C. (1984). "The Media, the War in Vietnam, and Political Support: A Critique of the Thesis of an Oppositional Media." *Journal of Politics*, vol. 46 (February): 2–24.

Hamilton, J. T. (2004). *All the News That's Fit to Sell: How the Market Transforms Information Into News*. Princeton, NJ: Princeton University Press.

Han, L. C. (2005). "The Rose Garden Strategy Revisited: How Presidents use Public Activities." In *The Public Domain: Presidents and the Challenges of Public Leadership*, edited by L. C. Han and D. J. Heith, 163–177. Albany: State University of New York Press.

Hansen, J. M. (1998). "Individuals, Institutions, and Public Preferences Over Public Finance." *American Political Science Review*, vol. 92: 513–531.

Hanson, D. M. (2004). "The High Priest of American Civil Religion: An Analysis of Religious Content in Presidential Inaugural Addresses" Paper presented at the annual meeting of the Western Political Science Association, Marriott Hotel, Portland, Oregon Online.

Havrilesky, T. (1995). *The Pressures on American Monetary Policy*. Boston: Springer Press.

Havrilesky, T. M., and Gildea, J. A. (1992). "Reliable and Unreliable Partisan Appointees to the Board of Governors." *Public Choice*, vol. 73: 397–418.

Hibbs, D. (1987). *The American Political Economy: Macroeconomics and Electoral Politics*. Cambridge, MA: Harvard University Press.

Hoffman, D. R., and Howard, A. D. (2010). "The Presidential Rhetoric of Hard Times." APSA 2010 Annual Meeting Paper. Available at SSRN: ssrn.com/abstract=1643794

———. (2006). *Addressing the State of the Union: The Evolution and Impact of the President's Big Speech*. Boulder, CO: Lynne Rienner Publishers.

Holbrook, R. A., and Hill, T. G. (2005). "Agenda-Setting and Priming in Prime Time Television: Crime Dramas as Political Cues." *Political Communication*, vol. 22: 277–295.

Holian, D. B. (2004). "He's Stealing My Issues! Clinton's Crime Rhetoric and the Dynamics of Issue Ownership." *Political Behavior*, vol. 26, no. 2: 95–124.

Hood, C. (1983). *The Tools of Government*. Chatham, NJ: Chatham House.

Hopkins, D. J., and King, G. (2010). "Automated Nonparametric Content Analysis for Social Science." *American Journal of Political Science*, vol. 54, no. 1 (January): 229–247.

Houck, D. W. (2001). *Rhetoric as Currency: Hoover, Roosevelt, and the Great Depression*. College Station: Texas A&M Univetsity Press.

Howell, W. G. (2003). *Power without Persuasion: The Politics of Direct Presidential Action*. Princeton, NJ: Princeton University Press.

Hurwtiz, J. (1989). "Presidential Leadership and Public Followership." In *Manipulating Public Opinion: Essays on Public Opinion as a Dependent Variable*, edited by Michael Margolis and Gary Mauser, 222–249. Boston: Harcourt.

Iyengar, S., and Kinder, D. R. (1987). *News That Matters: Television and American Opinion*. Chicago: University of Chicago Press.

Jacobs, L. R., and Shapiro, R. Y. (2000). *Politicians Don't Pander: Political Manipulation and the Loss of Democratic Responsiveness*. Chicago, IL: University of Chicago Press.

Jacobson, G. C. (2000). "Party Polarization in National Politics: The Electoral Connection." In *Polarized Politics: Congress and the President in a Partisan Era*, edited by J. Bond and R. Fleisher, 9–30. Washington, DC: Congressional Quarterly Press.

Jarvis, S. E., and Jones, E. B. (2005). "Party Labels in Presidential Acceptance Addresses: 1948–2000." In *The Public Domain: Presidents and the Challenges of Public Leadership*, edited by Lori Cox Han and Diane J. Heith, 29–48. Albany: State University of New York.

Jeong, G. H., Miller, G. J., and Sobel, A. (2008). "Political Compromise and Bureaucratic Structure: The Political Origins of the Federal Reserve System." *Journal of Law, Economics, and Organization*, vol. 25, no. 2: 472–498.

Jones, C. O. (1998). *The Passages to the Presidency: From Campaigning to Governing.* Washington, DC: Brookings Institute Press.

———. (1994). *The Presidency in a Separated System.* Washington, DC: Brookings Institution.

Kamlet, M. S., and Mowery, D. C. (September 1985). *Economic, political and institutional influences on executive and congressional budgetary priorities. /953-/98/.* Mimeo. 52 pp.

———. (1983). "Budgetary Side Payments and Government Growth: 1953–1968." *American Journal of Political Science*, vol. 63: 636–663.

Kalb, D., Peters, G. and Woolley, J. T. (2006). *State of the Union: Presidential Rhetoric from Woodrow Wilson to George W. Bush.* Washington, DC: Congressional Quarterly Press.

Kassop, N. (2005). "Not Going Public: George W. Bush and the Presidential Records Act." In *The Public Domain: Presidents and the Challenges of Public Leadership*, edited by L. C. Han and D. J. Heith, 255–278. Albany: State University of New York Press.

Keech, W. R., and Morris, I. L. (1997). "Appointments, Presidential Power, and the Federal Reserve." *Journal of Macroeconomics*, vol. 19, no. 2 (Spring): 253–267.

Kernell, S. (2007). *Going Public: New Strategies of Presidential Leadership*, 3rd Edition. Washington, DC: Congressional Quarterly Press.

Kiewiet, R. D. (1983). *Macroeconomics and Micropolitics: The Electoral Effects of Economic Issues.* Chicago, IL: University of Chicago Press.

Kiewiet, R. D., and McCubbins, M. D. (1985). "Appropriational Decisions as a Bilateral Bargaining Game Between President and Congress." *Legislative Studies Quarterly*, vol. 10: 181–201.

———. (1983). *The Effect of Economic Conditions, Parties, and Elections Upon the Congressional Appropriations Process.* Mimeo.

King, D. C. (1994). *Turf Wars: How Congressional Committees Claim Jurisdiction.* Chicago, IL: University of Chicago Press.

King, G., and Ragsdale L. (1988). *The Elusive Executive: Discovering Statistical Patterns in the Presidency.* Washington, DC: Congressional Quarterly Press.

Kingdon, J. (1999). *America the Unusual.* New York: Worth Publishers, Inc.

———. (1995). *Agendas, Alternatives, and Public Policies*, 2nd Edition. Boston: Little, Brown.

Kiplinger. (2014). *The Economy Since 9/11.* The Kiplinger Washington Editors.

Krause, G. A. (1994). "Federal Reserve Policy Decision Making: Political and Bureaucratic Influences." *American Journal of Political Science*, vol. 38, no. 1 (Feb.): 124–144.

Krehbiel, K. (1998). *Pivotal Politics: A Theory of U.S. Lawmaking.* Chicago, IL: University of Chicago Press.

———. (1991). *Information and Legislative Organization.* Ann Arbor: University of Michigan Press.

Krippendorff, K. (1970). "Reliability of Binary Attribute Data." *Biometrics*, vol. 34, no. 1: 142–144.

Krosnick, J. A., and Brannon, L. A. (1993). "The Impact of the Gulf War on the Ingredients of Presidential Evaluations: Multidimensional Effects of Political Involvement." *American Political Science Review*, vol. 87, no. 4: 963–975.

Kuklinski, J. H., and Hurley, N. L. (1996). "It's a Matter of Interpretation." In *Political Persuasion and Attitude Change*, edited by D. C. Mutz, P. M. Sniderman, and R. A. Brody, 125–144. Ann Arbor: University of Michigan Press.

Lakoff, G. (1987). *Women, Fire, and Dangerous Things: What Categories Reveal about the Mind*. Chicago, IL: University of Chicago Press.

Larcey, M. (1989). "The Presidential Newspaper: The Forgotten Way of Going Public." In *Speaking to the People: The Rhetorical Presidency in Historical Perspective*, edited by R. J. Ellis, 66–86. Amherst: University of Massachusetts Press.

Lau, R., and Redlawsk, D. (2006). *How Voters Decide: Information Processing during Election Campaigns*. New York: Cambridge University Press.

Lawrence, A. (2004). *Does It Matter What Presidents Say? The Influence of Presidential Rhetoric on the Public Agenda, 1946–2003*. Published Doctoral Dissertation at the University of Pittsburgh.

Leuchtenburg, W. (1995). *The Supreme Court Reborn: The Constitutional Revolution in the Age of Roosevelt*. Oxford, UK: Oxford University Press.

Light, P. (1999). *The President's Agenda: Domestic Policy Choice from Kennedy to Clinton*. Baltimore, MD: Johns Hopkins University Press.

Lim, E. T. (2008). *The Anti-Intellectual Presidency: The Decline of Presidential Rhetoric from George Washington to George W. Bush*. New York: Oxford University Press.

Lockerbie, B. (2008). *Do Voters Look to the Future?: Economics and Elections*. Albany: State University of New York Press.

Lohr, S. (2010). *Sampling: Design and Analysis*. Boston: Brooks/Cole Cengage Learning.

Long, J. S., and Freese, J. (2003). *Regression Models for Categorical Dependent Variables Using Stata*, revised edition. College Station, TX: Stata Press.

Lowi, T. (1985). *The Personal President: Power Invested, Promise Unfulfilled*. Ithaca, NY: Cornell University Press.

Lowry, W., and Shipan, C. (2002). "Party Differentiation in Congress." *Legislative Studies Quarterly*, vol. 27, no. 1 (February): 33–60.

MacDonald, J. A. (2010). "Limitation Riders and Congressional Influence over Bureaucratic Policy Decisions." *American Political Science Review*, vol. 104, no. 4: 766–782.

Maggio, J. (2007). "The Presidential Rhetoric of Terror: The (Re)Creation of Reality Immediately after 9/11." *Politics and Policy*, vol. 35, no. 4 (2007): 810–835.

Maisel, S. J. (1973). *Managing the Dollar: An Inside View by a Recent Governor of the Federal Reserve Board*. New York: W. W. Norton and Company.

Mayhew, D. (1989). "Does It Make a Difference Whether Party Control of the American National Government Is Unified or Divided?" (Paper presented at the annual meeting of the American Political Science Association, Atlanta, GA).

McGraw, K. M., and Hubbard, C. (1996). "Some of the People Some of the Time: Individual Differences in Acceptance of Political Accounts." In *Political Persuasion and Attitude Change*, edited by D. C. Mutz, P. M. Sniderman, and R. A. Brody, 145–170. Ann Arbor: University of Michigan Press.

Medhurst, M. J. (2007). "Rhetorical Leadership and the Presidency: A Situational Taxonomy." In *The Values of Presidential Leadership*, edited by T. L. Price and J. T. Wren, 59–84. New York: Palgrave Macmillan.

Miller, J. M., and Krosnick, J. A. (2000). "News Media Impact on the Ingredients of Presidential Evaluations: Politically Knowledgeable Citizens Are Guided by a Trusted Source." *American Journal of Political Science*, vol. 44: 295–309.

———. (1996). "News Media Impact on the Ingredients of Presidential Evaluations: A Program of Research on the Priming Hypothesis." In *Political Persuasion and Attitude Change*, edited by D. C. Mutz, P. M. Sniderman, and R. A. Brody, 79–100. Ann Arbor: University of Michigan Press.

Mondak, J. (1993). "Source Cues and Policy Approval: The Cognitive Dynamics of Public Support for the Reagan Agenda." *American Journal of Political Science*, vol. 37: 186–212.

Mondak, J. J., Mutz, D. C., and Huckfeldt, R. (1996). "Persuasion in Context: The Multilevel Structure of Economic Evaluations." In *Political Persuasion and Attitude Change*, edited by D. C. Mutz, P. M. Sniderman, and R. A. Brody, 249–266. Ann Arbor: University of Michigan Press.

Morris, I. (2000). *Congress, the President, and the Federal Reserve*. Ann Arbor: University of Michigan Press.

Morris, I., and Munger, M. (1998). "First Branch, or Root? The Congress, the President, and the Federal Reserve." *Public Choice*, vol. 96: 363–380.

Munger, M. C., and Roberts, B. E. (1990). "The Federal Reserve and Its Institutional Environment: A Review." In *The Political Economy of American Monetary Policy*, edited by Thomas Mayer, 83–98. Cambridge, UK: Cambridge University Press.

Murphy, J. M. (2009). "Political Economy and Rhetorical Matter." *Rhetoric and Public Affairs*, vol. 12: 303–315.

Mutz, D. C., Sniderman, P. M., and Brody, R. A. (eds.). (1996). *Political Persuasion and Attitude Change*. Ann Arbor: University of Michigan Press.

Nathan, R. (1983). *The Administrative Presidency*, 2nd Edition. New York: Wiley.

Nelson, M., and Riley, R. (2010). *The President's Words: Speeches and Speechwriting in the Modern White House*. Lawrence: University Press of Kansas.

Neustadt, R. (1991). *Presidential Power and the Modern Presidents: The Politics of Leadership from Roosevelt to Reagan*. New York: The Free Press.

Niskanen, W. A. (1971). *Bureaucracy and Representative Government*. Chicago, IL: Aldine-Atherton.

Nordhause, W. (1975). "The Political Business Cycle." *Review of Economic Studies*, vol. 42, no, 2 (April): 169–190.

Pack, J. R. (1988). "The Congress and Fiscal Policy." *Public Choice*, vol. 58 (August): 101–122.

Page, B. I., and Shapiro, R. Y. (1992). *The Rational Public: Fifty Years of Trends of Americans' Policy Preferences*. Chicago: University of Chicago Press.

———. (1982). "Changes in Americans' Policy Preferences, 1935–1979." *Public Opinion Quarterly*, vol. 46: 24–42.

Page, B. I., Shapiro, R. Y., and Dempsey, G. R. (1987). "What moves public opinion?" *American Political Science Review*, vol. 81: 23–43.

Peake, J. S. (2001). "Presidential Agenda Setting in Foreign Policy." *Political Research Quarterly*, vol. 54 (March): 69–86.

Peterson, M. A. (1990). *Legislating Together: The White House and Capitol Hill from Eisenhower to Reagan*. Cambridge, MA: Harvard University Press.

Pfiffner, J. (2001). "Deficit Reduction in 1993: Clinton's First Budget." In *Triumphs and Tragedies of the Modern Presidency: Seventy-Six Case Studies in Presidential Leadership*, edited by David Abshire. Center for the Study of the Presidency. Washington, DC: Praeger.

———. (1991). "Divided Government and the Problem of Governance." In *Divided Democracy: Cooperation and Conflict Between the President and Congress*, edited by J. Thurber. Washington, DC: Congressional Quarterly Press.

Polletta, F., and Ho, K. (2006). "Frames and their Consequences." In *The Oxford Handbook of Contextual Political Studies*, edited by Robert E. Goodin and Charles Tilly. New York: Oxford University Press.

Prais, S. J., and Winsten, C. B. (1954). "Trend Estimators and Serial Correlation." Cowles Commission Discussion Paper No. 383.Ragsdale, L. (1987). "Presidential Speechmaking and the Public Audience: Individual Presidents and Group Attitudes." *Journal of Politics*, vol. 49: 704–736.

Riffe, D., Lacy, S., and Fico, F. (2005). *Analyzing Media Messages: Using Quantitative Content Analysis in Research*. Hillsdale, NJ: Erlbaum Publishers.

Ritter, K., and Medhurst, M. J. (Ed). (2003). *Presidential Speechwriting: From the New Deal to the Reagan Revolution and Beyond*. College Station: Texas A&M University Press.

Rivers, D., and Rose, N. L. (1985). "Passing the President's Program: Public Opinion and Presidential Influence in Congress." *American Journal of Political Science*, vol. 29: 183–96.

Rockman, B. A. (1984). *The Leadership Question: The Presidency and the American System*. New York: Praeger.

Rose, R. (1991). *The Postmodern President*, 2nd Edition. Chatham, NJ: Chatham House.

Rosen, Corey M. (1973). "A Test of Presidential Leadership of Public Opinion: The Split-Ballot Technique." *Polity*, vol. 6: 282–290.

Sabatier, P., and Jenkins-Smith, H. (1999). "The Advocacy Coalition Framework." In *Theories of the Policy Process*, edited by P. Sabatier and H. Jenkins-Smith, 117–163. Boulder, CO: Westview Press.

Saeki, M. (2008). "Appointing the Fed Chair: The Political Influence of Presidential Appointment on the Federal Reserve Board in the United States." *Journal of Public Policy and Administration*, vol. 23, no. 3: 227–245.

Saeki, M., and Shull, S. A. (2003). "Who Influences the Fed? Presidential Verses Congressional Leadership." *Journal of Public Policy*, vol. 23, no. 3 (September): 261–278.

Schattschneider, E. E. (1960). *The Semi-Sovereign People: A Realist's View of Democracy in America*. New York: Holt.

Schlesinger, R. (2008). *White House Ghosts: Presidents and their Speechwriters*. New York: Simon and Schuster.

Schleuder, J., McCombs, M., and Wanta, W. (1991). "Inside the Agenda-Setting Process: How Political Advertising and TV News Prime Viewers to Think about Issues and Candidates." In *Television and Political Advertising: Vol. 1*, edited by F. Biocca, 265–309. Hillsdale, NJ: Lawrence Erlbaum.

Shapiro, I., Skowronek, S., and Galvin, D. (2006). *Rethinking Political Institutions: The Art of the State*. New York: New York University Press.

Sheingate, A. D. (2003). "Political eEntrepreneurship, Institutional Change, and American Political Development." *Studies in American Political Development*, vol. 17 (Fall): 185–203.

Shull, B. (2005). *The Fourth Branch: The Federal Reserve's Unlikely Rise to Power and Influence*. Westport, CT: Praeger Publishers and Greenwood Press.

Sigelman, L., and Rosenblatt, A. (1996). "Methodological Considerations in the Analysis of Presidential Persuasion." In *Political Persuasion and Attitude Change*, edited D. C. Mutz, P. M. Sniderman, and R. A, 171–194. Brody. Ann Arbor: University of Michigan Press.

Smith, C. A. (1983). "The Audience of the 'Rhetorical Presidency': An Analysis of President-Constituent Interactions." *Presidential Studies Quarterly*, vol. 8: 613–622.

Smith, S. S., and Deering, C. J. (1990). *Committees in Congress*, 2nd edition. Washington, DC: CQ Press.

Spriggs II, J. F. (1996). "The Supreme Court and Federal Administrative Agencies." *American Journal of Political Science*, vol. 40: 1122–1151.

Stein, H. (1994). *Presidential Economics: The Making of Economic Policy from Roosevelt to Clinton*. Washington, DC: The AEI Press.

Tackach, J. (2002). *Lincoln's Moral Vision: The Second Inaugural Address*. Jackson: University Press of Mississippi.

Teten, R. (2003). "Evolution of the Modern Rhetorical Presidency: Presidential Presentation and Development of the State of the Union Address." *Presidential Studies Quarterly*, vol. 33, no. 2: 333–346.

Thomas, D., and Sigelman, L. (1985). "Presidential Identification and Policy Leadership: Experimental Evidence on the Reagan Case." In *The Presidency and Public Policy Making*, edited by George C. Edwards III, Steven A. Shull, and Norman C. Thomas, 37–49. Pittsburgh, PA: University of Pittsburgh Press.

Thurber, J. (ed.). (2009). *Rivals for Power: Presidential Congressional Relations*. Lanham, MD: Rowman and Littlefield Publishers, Inc.

———. (ed.). (1991). *Divided Democracy: Cooperation and Conflict between the President and Congress*. Washington, DC: Congressional Quarterly Press.

Trager, R., and Vavreck, L. (2011). "The Political Costs of Crisis Bargaining: Presidential Rhetoric and the Role of Party." *American Journal of Political Science*, vol. 55, no. 3: 526–545.

Travis, N., Ridout, T. N., and Mellen Jr., R. (2007). "Does the Media Agenda Reflect the Candidates' Agenda?" *Harvard International Journal of Press/Politics*, vol. 12: 44–62.

Tufte, E. (1978). *Political Control of the Economy*. Princeton, NJ: Princeton University Press.

Tulis, J. K. (2008). "On the Forms of Rhetorical Leadership." In *Before the Rhetorical Presidency*, edited by M. J. Medhurst, 29–34. College Station, TX: Texas A&M University Press.

———. (2007). "The Rhetorical Presidency in Retrospect." *Critical Review*, vol. 19, no. 2: 3.

———. (1996). "Revising the Rhetorical Presidency." In *Beyond the Rhetorical Presidency*, edited by M. J. Medhurst, 3–14. College Station: Texas A&M University Press.

———. (1989). "Reflections on the Rhetorical Presidency in American Political Development." In *Speaking to the People: The Rhetorical Presidency in Historical Perspective*, edited by R. J. Ellis, 211–222. Amherst: University of Massachusetts Press.

———. (1987). *The Rhetorical Presidency*. Princeton, NJ: Princeton University Press.

Vavreck, L. (2009). *The Message Matters: The Economy and Presidential Campaigns*. Princeton, NJ: Princeton University Press.

Waldman, M. (2003). *My Fellow Americans: The Most Important Speeches of America's Presidents, from George Washington to George W. Bush*. Naperville, IL: Sourcebooks, Inc.

Waller, C. J. (1992). "A Bargaining Model of Partisan Appointment to the Central Bank." *Journal of Monetary Economics*, vol. 29 (June): 411–428.

Warber, A., and Olson, L. (2006). "Religion and the Public Presidency." A paper prepared for presentation at the American Political Science Association Meetings. Philadelphia, PA.

———. (2006). "Religious Rhetoric and the American Presidency." A paper prepared for presentation at the Midwest Political Science Association Meetings. Chicago, IL.

Waterman, R. (1989). *Presidential Influence and the Administrative State*. Knoxville: University of Tennessee Press.

Weintraub, R. E. (1978). "Congressional Supervision of Monetary Policy." *Journal of Monetary Economics*, vol. 4 (April): 341–362.

Welch, R. (2000). "Is Anybody Watching? The Audience for Televised Presidential Addresses." *Congress and the Presidency*, vol. 27: 41–58.

Welch, R. L. (2003). "Presidential Success in Communicating with the Public through Televised Addresses." *Presidential Studies Quarterly*, vol. 33: 347–65.

Whitford, A., and Ochs, H. (2006). "Political Roots of Executive Clemency." *American Politics Research*, vol. 34 (October): 825.

Whitford, A., and Yates, J. (2009). *Presidential Rhetoric and the Public Agenda: Constructing the War on Drugs*. Baltimore, MD: Johns Hopkins University Press.

Wildavsky, A. B., and Caiden, N. (2003). *New Politics of the Budgetary Process*, 5th Edition. Boston: Longman.

Windt Jr., T. O. (1986). "Presidential Rhetoric: Definition of a Field of Study." *Presidential Studies Quarterly*, vol. 16: 102–116.

Wlezien, C. (1995). "The Public as Thermostat: Dynamics of Preferences for Spending." *American Journal of Political Science*, vol. 39, no. 4: 981–1000.

Wolf, M., and Holian, D. (2006). "Polls, Elite Opinion, and the President: How Information and Issue Saliency Affect Approval." *Presidential Studies Quarterly*, vol. 36, no. 4 (December): 584–605.

Wood, B. D. (2012). *Presidential Saber Rattling: Causes and Consequences*. New York: Cambridge University Press.

———. (2007). *The Politics of Economic Leadership: The Causes and Consequences of Presidential Rhetoric*. Princeton, NJ: Princeton University Press.

———. (2004). "Presidential Rhetoric and Economic Leadership." *Presidential Studies Quarterly*, vol. 34: 573–606.

Wood, B., and Peake, J. (1998). "The Dynamics of Foreign Policy Agenda Setting." *American Political Science Review*, vol. 92: 173–184.

Wood, B. D., and Waterman, R. W. (1994). *Bureaucratic Dynamics*. Boulder, CO: Westview Press, Inc.

Wood, D., Owens, T., and Durham, B. (2005). "Presidential Rhetoric and the Economy." *Journal of Politics*, vol. 67, no. 3: 627–645.

Woods, J. (2011). "Framing Terror: An Experimental Framing Effects Study of the Perceived Threat of Terrorism." *Critical Studies on Terrorism*, vol. 4, no. 2, (August): 199–217.

Woods, J., and Arthur, C. D. (2014). "The Threat of Terrorism and the Changing Public Discourse on Immigration after September 11." *Sociological Spectrum* (Forthcoming Sept/Oct 2014).

Woolley, J. T. and Peters, J. (2014). *The American Presidency Project* [online]. Santa Barbara: University of California. Available from World Wide Web: www.presidency.ucsb.edu.

———. Barack Obama: "Inaugural Address," January 20, 2009. Online by Gerhard Peters and John T. Woolley, *The American Presidency Project*. www.presidency.ucsb.edu/ws/?pid=44.

———. Barack Obama: "Statement from Senator Obama Commending Federal Regulators on Blocking Golden Parachutes for Fannie Mae and Freddie Mac CEOs," September 15, 2008. Online by Gerhard Peters and John T. Woolley, *The American Presidency Project*. www.presidency.ucsb.edu/ws/?pid=91050.

———. Franklin D. Roosevelt: "Excerpts from the Press Conference," July 23, 1937. Online by Gerhard Peters and John T. Woolley, *The American Presidency Project*. www.presidency.ucsb.edu/ws/?pid=15439.

———. George W. Bush: "Address to the Nation on the Terrorist Attacks," September 11, 2001. Online by Gerhard Peters and John T. Woolley, *The American Presidency Project*. www.presidency.ucsb.edu/ws/?pid=58057.

———. George W. Bush: "Remarks in a Meeting with the National Security Team and an Exchange With Reporters at Camp David, Maryland," September 15, 2001. Online by Gerhard Peters and John T. Woolley, *The American Presidency Project*. www.presidency.ucsb.edu/ws/?pid=63199.

———. George W. Bush: "Remarks on Arrival at the White House and an Exchange with Reporters," September 16, 2001. Online by Gerhard Peters and John T. Woolley, *The American Presidency Project*. www.presidency.ucsb.edu/ws/?pid=63346.

———. George W. Bush: "Remarks to Employees in the Pentagon and an Exchange with Reporters in Arlington, Virginia," September 17, 2001. Online by Gerhard Peters and John T. Woolley, *The American Presidency Project*. www.presidency.ucsb.edu/ws/?pid=65079.

———. George W. Bush: "Address before a Joint Session of the Congress on the United States Response to the Terrorist Attacks of September 11," September 20, 2001. Online by Gerhard Peters and John T. Woolley, *The American Presidency Project*. www.presidency.ucsb.edu/ws/?pid=64731.

———. George W. Bush: "The President's Radio Address," September 22, 2001. Online by Gerhard Peters and John T. Woolley, *The American Presidency Project*. www.presidency.ucsb.edu/ws/?pid=25000.

———. George W. Bush: "Remarks on United States Financial Sanctions Against Terrorists and Their Supporters and an Exchange with Reporters," September 24, 2001. Online by Gerhard Peters and John T. Woolley, *The American Presidency Project*. www.presidency.ucsb.edu/ws/?pid=64040.

———. George W. Bush: "Remarks to Airline Employees in Chicago, Illinois," September 27, 2001. Online by Gerhard Peters and John T. Woolley, *The American Presidency Project*. www.presidency.ucsb.edu/ws/?pid=65084.

———. George W. Bush: "Remarks Following a Meeting with Congressional Leaders and an Exchange with Reporters," October 2, 2001.Online by Gerhard Peters and John T. Woolley, *The American Presidency Project*. www.presidency.ucsb.edu/ws/?pid=65085.

———. George W. Bush: "The President's Radio Address," December 1, 2001. Online by Gerhard Peters and John T. Woolley, *The American Presidency Project*. www.presidency.ucsb.edu/ws/?pid=24990.

———. Herbert Hoover: "Annual Message to the Congress on the State of the Union," December 2, 1930. Online by Gerhard Peters and John T. Woolley, *The American Presidency Project*. www.presidency.ucsb.edu/ws/?pid=22458.

———. Lyndon B. Johnson: "Remarks in Chicago before the National Association of Broadcasters," April 1, 1968. Online by Gerhard Peters and John T. Woolley, *The American Presidency Project*. www.presidency.ucsb.edu/ws/?pid=28774.

———. Richard Nixon: "Remarks at the Swearing In of Dr. Arthur F. Burns as Chairman of the Board of Governors of the Federal Reserve System," January 31, 1970.

Online by Gerhard Peters and John T. Woolley, *The American Presidency Project*. www.presidency.ucsb.edu/ws/?pid=2569.

———. Richard Nixon: "The President's News Conference," August 4, 1971. Online by Gerhard Peters and John T. Woolley, *The American Presidency Project*. www.presidency.ucsb.edu/ws/?pid=3100.

———. Ronald Reagan: "Address before the Assembly of the Republic of Portugal in Lisbon," May 9, 1985. Online by Gerhard Peters and John T. Woolley, *The American Presidency Project*. www.presidency.ucsb.edu/ws/?pid=38605.

———. William J. Clinton: "Address before a Joint Session of Congress on Administration Goals," February 17, 1993. Online by Gerhard Peters and John T. Woolley, *The American Presidency Project*. www.presidency.ucsb.edu/ws/?pid=47232.

———. William J. Clinton: "Remarks in the 'CBS This Morning' Town Meeting," May 27, 1993. Online by Gerhard Peters and John T. Woolley, *The American Presidency Project*. www.presidency.ucsb.edu/ws/?pid=46624.

———. William J. Clinton: "Remarks on Senate Action on the Economic Program," August 6, 1993. Online by Gerhard Peters and John T. Woolley, *The American Presidency Project*. www.presidency.ucsb.edu/ws/?pid=46963.

Worsham, J. (2006). "Up in Smoke: Mapping Subsystem Dynamics in Tobacco Policy." *Policy Studies Journal*, vol. 34, no. 3 (August): 437–452.

———. (1997). "Doing the Subsystem Two-Step." *Other People's Money*. Boulder, CO: Westview Press.

Yates, J., and Whitford, A. (2005). "Institutional Foundations of the President's Issue Agenda." *Political Research Quarterly*, vol. 58, no. 4 (December): 577–585.

Young, G., and Perkins, W. B. (2005). "Presidential Rhetoric, the Public Agenda, and the End of Presidential Television's 'Golden Age.'" *Journal of Politics*, vol. 67: 1190–1205.

Zaller, J. (1998). "Monica Lewinsky's Contribution to Political Science." *PS: Political Science and Politics*, vol. 31, no. 2: 182–189.

———. (1998). "Monica Lewinsky's Contribution to Political Science." *PS: Political Science and Politics*, vol. 31, no. 2: 182–189.

———. (1996). "The Myth of Massive Media Impact Revived: New Support for a Discredited Idea." In *Political Persuasion and Attitude Change*, edited by D. C. Mutz, P. M. Sniderman, and R. A. Brody, 17–78. Ann Arbor: University of Michigan Press.

———. (1992). *The Nature and Origins of Mass Opinion*. Cambridge, UK: Cambridge University Press.

———. (1991). "Information, Values, and Opinion." *American Political Science Review*, vol. 85, no. 4 (December): 1215–1237.

———. (1987). "Diffusion of Political Attitudes." *Journal of Personality and Social Psychology*, vol. 53, no. 5: 821–833.

Zarefsky, D. (2004). "Presidential Rhetoric and the Power of Definition." *Presidential Studies Quarterly*, vol. 34: 607–619.

Index

About the Author

C. Damien Arthur is an assistant professor of political science at West Virginia State University, a public land-grant and historically black university (HBCU). His research has focused upon, primarily, presidential rhetoric in relation to salient policies such as economics, institutional interaction, and immigration as well as religion. His most recent work has been published in *Presidential Studies Quarterly* and *Sociological Spectrum*.

He completed a PhD in political science at West Virginia University. He has an MA in American public policy and an MPA in public administration from West Virginia University. He also completed an MTS in religion, culture, and personality at Boston University's School of Theology, *magna cum laude*. He received a BA in theological studies from Gordon College in Wenham, MA.

www.ingramcontent.com/pod-product-compliance
Ingram Content Group UK Ltd.
Pitfield, Milton Keynes, MK11 3LW, UK
UKHW041627031026
15587UKWH00001B/116

9 780739 187838